Scandinavia

THE HORIZON CONCISE HISTORY OF
Scandinavia

by Ewan Butler

Published by
AMERICAN HERITAGE PUBLISHING CO., INC.
New York

Library of Congress Cataloging in Publication Data
Butler, Ewan.
    The Horizon concise history of Scandinavia.
    1. Scandinavia—History. 2. Finland—History.
I. Horizon (New York, 1958–   ). II. Title.
DL46.B88   948   73-2734
ISBN 0-07-009365-2

Introduction

The term "Scandinavia" is simply a matter of convenience. It has no meaning in a political sense, and it is no more than a blanket description of four nations of northern Europe. (Some people insist upon including Iceland, making a total of five nations, but we shall not do so in this book.) Denmark, Norway, Sweden, and Finland, the four countries with which we are here concerned, cover an area of about 445,000 square miles with a combined population today of somewhat more than twenty million. Scandinavia, therefore, has roughly one eighth of the area of the United States and about a tenth of her population.

Three of the four Scandinavian nations share what is virtually a common language, although Danish differs more in structure and, above all, in pronunciation from Swedish and Norwegian than those two languages do from one another. The Finns are the odd men out in this Scandinavian family. Their extremely difficult tongue has an affinity with no other European languages except those of the Hungarians, Lapps, and Estonians, to whom they are related by race.

It might be thought that at least Sweden, Norway, and Denmark, speaking something like a common language and being close neighbors, would long ago have united in a federation, such as Switzerland (with its French-, German-, and Italian-speaking populations) has managed to establish. This idea has been put forward for many centuries and more than one attempt to create such a union has been made, but never with any long-lasting success. Even today, when it might seem that a federation of some kind was more urgently needed than ever before, if only for common defense or economic survival, agreement is as elusive as ever. Denmark and Norway, for example, are members of NATO. Sweden prefers to "go it alone." The reasons for this continuing exclusiveness lie in the history and geography of Scandinavia; it is hoped that this book will to some extent explain them.

Water is the most important geographical feature in the lives of all Scandinavians. Norway has a coastline 1,650 miles long, with no fewer than 150,000 islands scattered along it. Sweden with its extensive coastline also boasts 96,000 lakes, and Finland 60,000, covering one tenth of the country's area. Denmark consists of a large European peninsula and an archipelago dividing the North Sea from the Baltic.

Sweden is the largest of the Scandinavian countries and the fourth largest in Europe, its 173,000 square miles exceeded only by European Russia, France, and Spain. With eight million people Sweden is also the most populous of the Scandinavian nations, although this reduces to a relatively sparse forty-nine inhabitants per square mile.

Still more thinly populated is Norway—indeed its people-to-area ratio is the lowest in Europe, with 3,900,000 inhabitants spread across 125,000 square miles for a density of thirty-one Norwegians per square mile. The land mass, 1,090 miles in length, is mostly long and narrow —only four miles across at its narrowest point—between the Swedish frontier and the sea with a bulbous mass at its southwestern end. The warm North Atlantic Drift Current ensures that Norway's coast is free of ice at all seasons, and this blessing has enabled the Norwegians to build up their remarkable merchant navy, which now accounts for one tenth of the world's total tonnage.

Winter and summer, coastal steamers ply a 1,200-mile route between Bergen in the south and Kirkenes in the far north, and the round trip takes twelve days. The ships link hundreds of tiny, isolated villages and hamlets standing on long, deep bays, or fjords (the longest of them penetrating 114 miles inland), and on the thousands of islands which lie off the Norwegian coast. Until the coming of steamships and, now, of aircraft, the sea split Norway into hundreds of small communities which were cut off from one another by water and by mountains, and this isolation has profoundly influenced the Norwegian people.

The smallest of the Scandinavian nations, Denmark, is also the most densely populated. Its 17,000 square miles—slightly more than the area of Switzerland—support 4,900,000 people on the mainland of Jutland, six large islands (Zealand, Fyn, Bornholm, Langeland, and Falster and Lolland), and many smaller ones. Danish history has been largely governed by the fact that the Danish mainland has a common border with Germany. Unlike Sweden and Finland, which look out only upon the Baltic Sea, and Norway, which confronts the North Sea only, Denmark faces both the Baltic and the North seas, and this too has greatly affected the country's people and its place in the world.

Only since the Russian Revolution of 1918 has it been possible to number Finland among the independent nations. Throughout the whole of its earlier history Finland was ruled either by Sweden or by Russia, sometimes with a large measure of self-government, sometimes with none at all. Today Finland—the "Fenland," which Finns call *Suomi*—is a republic with 130,000 square miles of territory and 4,700,000 people. It has been described, with some justice, as "the most remote country in Europe," but it is also one of the most advanced of European nations in many aspects of civilization and now, with increased air travel, it is no longer physically remote either.

This abolition of distance, for which ever-quickening transportation, television, and radio are chiefly responsible, has also done much to create a common life style among Scandinavians. Nevertheless, the Danes, Norwegians, Swedes, and Finns persist in holding some long-standing prejudices about the peculiar "national characteristics" of their immediate neighbors. The Danes, for instance, will tell you that Swedes are stiff, cold, and snobbish. Swedes tend to deplore Danish "frivolity" and to look upon the Norwegians as an uncultured people. Norwegians and Finns pride themselves upon their toughness and think the Swedes and Danes soft and effete. And so on.

There is at least some foundation for all these beliefs, and it lies in the history of each country, and their interrelationships through the centuries. Of that history this book attempts to give a swift sketch.

CHAPTER I

OF ICE AND IRON

About ten thousand years before the birth of Christ northern Europe was still covered by an ice cap. The weight of these immense glaciers—some as thick as six thousand feet or more—caused much of the solid land to sink beneath the sea, only to rise again as the ice gradually melted; the region of Denmark was the first to become ice-free. In that distant past what are now the Danish islands were a continuous land mass, joining Denmark to what was to become southern Sweden. As the land gradually rose—in Finland it is still rising at the rate of approximately three feet each century—the sea came sweeping into the low ground, leaving the higher elevations as islands. There is evidence that man had penetrated to the coastal regions of the Arctic Ocean as early as 8000 B.C., but most of present-day Sweden, Norway, and Finland were still thinly peopled when tribes from southern Europe began to move into the region of Denmark in numbers about 2000 B.C. They were, like all the people of western Europe at this time, primitive hunting folk, using flint tools and weapons, and soon the venturers began to settle in Sweden also.

As the centuries passed, life became more civilized for these settlers,

These man-made earthen mounds of Old Uppsala are thought to be the funeral cairns of kings Aun, Egil, and Adils who ruled Sweden in the sixth century.

all of whom seem to have been of Germanic origins. A small Stone Age village which has been excavated at Alvastra, in Sweden, proves that its inhabitants sowed and harvested crops, domesticated cattle, pigs, and dogs, and were successful hunters and fishermen. Later, as man's knowledge advanced, and new waves of migratory peoples added their achievements to the accumulation of tribal skills, the Scandinavian peoples began to develop far-reaching trade. Especially important was the exchange of local goods for bronze, from as far away as Hungary, Spain, and France, and this brilliant Bronze Age lasted for about one thousand two hundred years, until 600 B.C. Cliff drawings from this period that have been discovered in Sweden show that the ancestors of the Swedish people used oxen for plowing, traveled in horse-drawn carts, and went to sea in ships driven by oarsmen.

The Iron Age, which succeeded that of bronze, brought great advantages to Scandinavia, for Sweden had and still has vast quantities of iron ore. Once this could be smelted it provided tools and weapons far better than any that had hitherto been possible. Little is known of the first part of this era, however, since the early Iron Age people seem to have preferred cremation to the burial rites of their forebears. (Bronze Age tomb furnishings give archaeologists their most useful clues to life in the period before history can be said to have really begun.) The Iron Age, which occupied the last five centuries before the birth of Christ, also seems to have brought to Denmark and southern Sweden bands of invading Celts, a more civilized central European people than the native inhabitants. These wanderers settled largely in Jutland, or the Cimbrian Peninsula as the Romans called it. A century before the birth of Christ these Cimbri spilled out of Denmark across Europe and at last reached Italy, where they were beaten by the Roman general Marius at Vercellae in 101 B.C. No doubt the remnants of this raiding force fought their way back to Jutland against hostile tribesmen, and the Cimbri did not, for a while, again venture abroad. However, a return engagement with the Romans is mentioned by Emperor Augustus, who claimed in an inscription attributed to him, "My fleet sailed from the mouth of the Rhine eastward to the country of the Cimbri, to which no Roman had ever penetrated before that time by sea or by land. . . ." This is the first official reference to what we now know as Denmark.

In the meanwhile, on the eastern side of the Baltic, another group of nomads was establishing itself: the Ugrians from the region of the Volga River were hunters, trappers, and fishermen. As they moved westward the tribe split into two groups, one of which trekked toward the south and became the ancestors of today's Hungarians. The other group, keeping to the north, established themselves in what is now Finland and Estonia. In their advance into Finland the Ugrian invaders settled among the Bronze Age people and drove north the native Lapps who retreated toward the Arctic Circle, where they have lived as a separate and distinct group ever since. The Roman historian Tacitus wrote that these Lapplanders were "extremely wild," a reputation which their descendants have done something to maintain, as the Soviet armies had cause to discover some thirty years ago.

Meanwhile, the dark, inhospitable coast of Norway had also become thinly colonized by western and central European immigrants who had come by way of Denmark, Sweden, and Russia. By the eighth century A.D. these settlers had found that their new, thickly forested homeland was altogether too bleak and unfertile for their tastes, which with the stimulation of developing trade and international communication had become more demanding.

Geography determined the direction in which the Northmen now struck. The land route toward the south was blocked in the ninth century by the great Frankish empire of Charlemagne and by the warlike Saxons; eastward and westward, however, the coast was, literally, clear. The Danes, closer to the English Channel than the Norwegians, attacked Frisia (corresponding roughly to the Netherlands), southern England, and France; the Norwegians swept out toward the Orkney and Shetland islands, the Isle of Man, Ireland, Scotland, and Northumbria; and the Swedes went east. The Finns enjoyed the benefits of Swedish commerce with the East but did not themselves launch any raids except upon the Lapps.

The term "Vikings" had been loosely applied to all these sea raiders, whether Danish, Swedish, or Norwegian, and it derives from the word *vik* which still means "creek" in all Scandinavian languages. The Vikings were "creekmen." Their long-ships lay hidden in creeks and bays, ready to swoop out against any passing vessel, and they used the waterways to penetrate the countryside which they intended to plunder.

"Norsemen" is simply an alternative name for these marauders, again applied to all three Scandinavian peoples. Normandy, settled by the Danes in 911, reminds us of the Norse origins of that duchy and to this day Norwegians refer to themselves as Nordmenn. (The Norse invaders of Russia are alternately known as Varangians, derived from an old Norse word, possibly meaning "confederate," and Ruotsi —meaning the "rowing men" in old Finnish.)

With the passage of time the raids were organized on a large scale until at last they became colonizing expeditions, carefully planned and skillfully executed. Because of their riches, English and Irish monasteries were always a prime target for the Vikings, and the people of the villages which clustered around the great religious houses learned to look fearfully toward the sea whence came, in the words of a monkish chronicler, "great armies of Norsemen like storm-clouds or swarms of grasshoppers." As the historian Adam of Bremen wrote of the Vikings in the tenth century, "Forced by the poverty of their

homeland they venture far into the world to bring back from their raids the goods which other countries so plentifully produce." Northern France and Iceland also learned to dread them.

The Vikings were democrats, in a sense. Great fleets of hundreds of long-ships were assembled for a large expedition without any single leader being in charge of the operation. "We are all equals," said the Norsemen proudly to the envoy of the king of France who came to Normandy inquiring for their leader, and there was some truth in this. Women were held in highest esteem by the Vikings and enjoyed rights of property and status which their sex was not to enjoy elsewhere until many centuries later.

What is known of the legal proceedings of Iceland during the Viking era is probably true in a general sense of the government of all the Nordic peoples. Laws derived from the decisions of the *Thing*—an assembly of landowning free men. Each district, of which there might be as many as a hundred in a given county, had its own assembly, and the judgments of the Thing were passed on orally from one generation to the next. Great regional assemblies, at which men from many districts came together—usually in the summer—considered such larger questions as the election of kings, the declaration of war, the religious conversion of the people. The first truly national Thing was called in Iceland in 930—and this Thing would meet annually almost without interruption until 1798. The great and chronic weakness of the Nordic Thing everywhere that it existed was its inability to implement its decisions. Legislative and judicial in character, it lacked executive power, and often its decisions—especially where individual complaints were involved—were ultimately settled by duel or some other violent means. Nevertheless, its democratic spirit would prove of abiding importance to the later development of Scandinavia.

The houses of a Viking township were mostly oval in floor plan, the roof supported by wooden pillars and with a hole at its peak to carry away the smoke from a central fireplace. They were rude dwellings, but warm and snug; the great mead hall of a local chieftain, at which a hundred retainers might sit down to dinner, was, by the standards of the time, an impressive building.

The people who lived in these settlements dressed well. In winter, men wore thick coats with long sleeves, trousers, and long cloaks, the

Stone tablets such as this have been found throughout Viking territory and bear inscriptions in the ancient runic alphabet.

Opposite, far left, are weapons of a Viking Warrior; left and above are thir-teenth-century Norse chessmen found in a sandhill in the Outer Hebrides.

women were clad in warm undergarments worn under sleeveless dresses and capes thrown back to expose the figure. As the Vikings' raids became more profitable and Swedish trade with the East increased, rich fabrics (Chinese silks, cloth of gold, and solid worsteds from the south have been found in Viking graves) became the fashion for all who could afford them, and personal jewelry a status symbol. Men wore gold and silver armbands, and women rings and necklaces, some made by local craftsmen, others imported. Viking burial places have also yielded a rich store of gold and silver cups and bowls, elaborately decorated harnesses, and memorial stones inscribed with runes—a primitive sixteen-letter alphabet used before the adoption of the Latin alphabet. Depictions of animals, as might be expected, played a great part in the art of the Norsemen, in particular a small catlike creature with curved paws which appears in dozens of surviving Viking carvings.

Weapons, of course, were all-important. Although the twin-bladed battle-axe has become the very symbol of Norse prowess in war, it was the sword, broad in the blade and heavy at the hilt, that was the chief pride of its owner, and many of the swords which survive are elegantly ornamented, often by Frankish swordsmiths and craftsmen. The Viking warrior went into battle in a mailed *serk,* or shirt, his head protected by a helmet of iron or leather and his body by a heavy circular shield. Sometimes a warrior threw away these protective devices and rushed into the fray naked from the waist up and armed only with a club. Such bold spirits were said to have "gone berserk," and if they lived through the battle they enjoyed special esteem ever afterward.

The last years of the eighth century saw the first full-scale Viking raids upon England and Ireland. In A.D. 793 an enormous force of Norsemen swept down upon the great island monastery of Lindisfarne off the Northumberland coast, sacked it, and slaughtered the monks. Every year that followed brought further raids, and it was not long before every Irish river estuary became the "kingdom" of some Norse chieftain who, with his band of warriors, held the district against all comers, for they found the countryside far more fertile and pleasant than their own homelands.

The Irish, peaceful Christian people as they then were, were no match for the cruel Norsemen. On one occasion Danes and Nor-

This nineteenth-century bronze sculpture by A. Stirling Calder depicts Leif Ericsson who reached the North American coast centuries before Columbus.

wegians fought a bitter battle against one another on Irish soil. (As has already been noted no idea of nationhood yet existed in Scandinavia and the battles between, say, Danes and Norwegians were episodes in a kind of tribal warfare.) When a deputation from the local Irish king called upon the victors they found that the Danes had lighted cooking fires among the piles of Norwegian corpses and set up their spits by driving stakes through the bodies of the dead.

Although Alfred the Great, king of the West Saxons, succeeded in holding the Danes off in southern England, all of Northumberland had fallen to other Danish aggressors by 876. To end the strife Alfred reached a compromise with one of their leaders by which that territory known as the Danelaw would remain uncontestedly Danish in exchange for the conversion of the invaders to Christianity. The new settlers soon became farmers. Likewise, the western European mainland—from France to Spain and to Italy via the Mediterranean—also suffered numerous Norse raids. After Paris had been besieged and a tribute exacted from the French king, the French and the Vikings came to terms. By a treaty signed in 911, the French relinquished a portion of the Frankish coast lying between Brittany and the Low Countries to the Norse chieftain Hrolf, or Rollo, who henceforth ruled it as the duchy of Normandy in return for nominal vassalage.

About this time we see the uniting of Norway's petty kingdoms under a single ruler, and the birth of the Norwegian nation. According to an ancient saga, a woman was responsible for this event, a certain Gyda who won the heart of Harold the Fairhaired, ruler of a small area of southern Norway. But Gyda had ambitions. She had no use, she told her suitor, for "little kings." Let Harold conquer all Norway and Gyda would be his queen. Vowing not to cut his mop of blond hair until he had fulfilled Gyda's bidding, Harold spent the next eight years battling, but a final victory over his rivals at Hafrs Fjord in 872 (recent scholarship places the date near 900) established him as undisputed king of all Norway. Gyda duly married her hero, who reigned over all Norway for some sixty years. Travelers today who approach Bergen by sea can hardly fail to see, as they pass the island of Haugesund, the monument of red granite, fifty feet high, which the Norwegians erected in 1872 to honor the 1000-year anniversary of the uniting of Norway.

The Låtefoss in Hordaland county is one of the countless waterfalls that link the glaciers and fjords of Norway.

Meanwhile, the hundred years from 850 to 950 were a time of great disturbance in Denmark, now more or less officially known by that name. Even Adam of Bremen, who lived shortly after and who was a conscientious historian, could not make any sense of that Danish century, and where he failed we, at a distance of some eleven hundred years, can hardly hope to succeed. We are told that no fewer than fifty kings ruled in Denmark during this period but, as old Adam says, "whether of all these kings or tyrants in Denmark some ruled the country at the same time or one lived shortly after the other is uncertain."

Of happenings in Sweden we know a good deal more. The two chief tribes there were the Sveas, from which Sweden takes its name, and the Gotar, or Goths. The early kings of Sweden, insofar as one can speak of Sweden as a country at this time, lived at Uppsala, where they and their people worshiped three chief gods: Thor, Odin, and Freya. The temple was a splendid place richly decorated with gold and there, every nine years, a great festival was held to which each tribe in Sweden sent delegates and at which animals and humans were sacrificed. Kingship, though, was rather a risky job, since if the harvests failed or plague broke out the people were quite likely to sacrifice their king as a specially flattering offering to the angry deities. In 829 Ansgar, a Benedictine monk, went to Sweden as the first official Christian missionary to the North and baptized one or two local chieftains in the district in which Stockholm now stands; but with no ministers to carry on his teachings, the churches which he founded were soon engulfed by the well-established system of pagan worship.

While the Danes and the Norwegians were venturing southward and westward in their search for a better life, the Swedes looked toward the East. Already, Swedish *Ruotsi,* or rowing men, had made themselves the masters of much of the eastern coast of the Baltic and had established settlements in what would later be called Finland, Estonia, Lithuania, and Latvia. But the Swedes were not content to remain on the Baltic coast. They rowed their long-ships down the gulf which leads to the modern Leningrad and up to Lake Ladoga, that great inland sea. Thence the Ruotsi, or "Rus" (as the Slav tribesmen they met corrupted the name), set the prows of their vessels toward the south, down the network of rivers that run to the Black and the Caspian seas. They were led, the Russian chroniclers tell us, by Rurik and two lieutenants, Askold and Dir, who were possibly his brothers. Rurik founded a "kingdom" south of Lake Ladoga and established the city of Novgorod, while his brothers, pressing farther south, set themselves up as kings of Kiev, on the Dnieper River. By the year 900 the two Swedish colonies were united as the lusty new state of Kievan Rus. Russia owes her name and her foundation as a nation to these Swedish oarsmen.

The purpose of the Swedes was not so much conquest, though that was an essential part of their plan, as trade. Swedish ships plied the river courses in such numbers that even Constantinople was threatened by the merchant-marauders. There, at the seat of the Roman Empire, the Swedes gathered goods from the East—gold, silver, carpets, tapestries, perfumes, leatherwork, dried fruits, precious stones, and many other things never before seen in their homeland. These treasures were shipped to Gotland, a large island in the middle of the southern Baltic

Scenes from an 1130 manuscript show the British king Edmund as a Danish hostage (left) and his adversary King Sven on a throne (right).

Sea, which developed into a rich trading entrepôt. To it came merchants from the mainland of Sweden, Denmark, and countries as far afield as France and Holland. Modern research has unearthed in Gotland hoards of coins from every part of the world known to tenth-century Europe.

In the year 940 the skies began to clear over Denmark. An energetic monarch named Harold Bluetooth made himself king of all Denmark, and twenty years later he was converted to Christianity, making Denmark the first Scandinavian country to renounce formally its ancient pagan faith. Bluetooth's long reign of almost fifty years ended when he was killed in battle against his son, Sven Forkbeard. The rebellious Sven proved an even more ambitious ruler, invading England and besieging London in 994, before he was bribed to go away by the English ruler Ethelred II, surnamed "the Unready."

Returning home, Sven found that Denmark had been seized in his absence by King Eric the Victorious, who was the ruler of a large part of Sweden. This was an occupational hazard which all monarchs of the time had to accept if they insisted on going abroad to fight their battles, but luckily for Sven Forkbeard Eric had died in the interim, leaving his son and heir, Olaf, who was a more accommodating character. Not only did Olaf of Sweden make peace with the Danish king, but he suggested that Sven might care to marry Eric's widow, an extremely masterful lady named, not without good reason, Sigrid the Proud.

Sigrid was looked upon as a good match, and the king of Norway, Olaf I Tryggvesson, also gave suit. Although the Norwegian was an extremely handsome young man—a chronicler describes him as "the most wildly beautifullest man in all the annals of Norway"—Sigrid could not agree with his religious views. Olaf Tryggvesson had been baptized a Christian during his campaigns in England, not because he felt much drawn toward the gospel or understood its meaning, but because to be a Christian was becoming fashionable and Olaf was anxious to keep up with the times. However, like many converts, Olaf was now extremely keen on his new faith and he insisted that Sigrid should be baptized before she marry him. The dowager queen, a thoroughgoing pagan, refused, whereupon Olaf struck her with his glove, shouting that she was "heathen like a dog." Drawing herself

This manuscript illustration shows a Danish raiding party landing in England.

up, Sigrid grimly retorted: "This will be your death," and she was quite right.

Sigrid promptly married Sven Forkbeard of Denmark and began to nag both her new husband and her son, Olaf of Sweden, to unite against Olaf Tryggvesson. This they did, and the combined fleets of Denmark and Sweden met the Norwegian fleet at Svöld, off the coast of the island of Rügen in the year 1000. Crowding two hundred axe-men and swordsmen aboard his flagship *Long Serpent,* built to carry a crew of thirty-four, Olaf Tryggvesson went into battle. Not surprisingly *Long Serpent* capsized and the Norwegian king drowned. Norway was divided between his conquerors, paganism was once again fully tolerated, and Sigrid felt that she had been avenged. A woman had persuaded Harold the Fairhaired to unite all Norway under his crown and now, 118 years later, a woman's promptings destroyed that unity and caused Norway to be torn apart.

Incidentally, the picturesque nicknames by which the Norsemen distinguished themselves from one another—Bluetooth, Forkbeard, Fairhaired, and so on—were very necessary in an age which knew no surnames as we understand them. Short on first names, they found it convenient to identify one another by their distinguishing physical or personality characteristics. (The passage of many centuries has not changed matters greatly. In modern Scandinavia, identical surnames are shared by a great number of people—permanent surnames were not required or widely used until the nineteenth century, at which time the majority of the people adopted patronymics: Petersen, Anderson, and the like.) A glance at the Stockholm telephone directory, for instance, will reveal column after column of Svenssons. These Svenssons are listed not in order of their first names, whose popular choices are also fairly narrow, but by profession. Thus, Svensson, Olaf, *Byggmästare* (a master builder), is listed ahead of Svensson, Bengt, *Tandläkare* (a dentist). Unless you know the profession of the Svensson (or Nilsson or Gustavsson or Olafsson) whom you are trying to call up you may have some difficulty in finding his number.

The troubled condition of Norway in the year 1000 may have driven a certain Leif Ericsson to undertake one of the world's most momentous voyages. The story begins in 986, so the Norse sagas tell us, when a seaman named Bjarni Herjolfsson sailed out of Norway and after a long and perilous passage by way of Iceland sighted the American continent. However, Bjarni and his crew continued on to Greenland, where they stayed for several years. But later Bjarni returned to Norway, telling of rich meadowland and forest waiting to be farmed and harvested by any men who had the courage to follow in the wake of their expedition. Tales of this fabulous "Vinland the Good" spread slowly among the Norwegian fjords and islands, and in the year 1001 Leif Ericsson bought Bjarni Herjolfsson's old ship and, with a crew of thirty-five, set sail for the promised land.

Steering westward from Greenland, Ericsson came upon an immense iceberg and set course southward, until at last he found his "Markland" (Forest Land), with fine grazing, rivers full of salmon, and immense stands of timber. Here, the sagas say, the Vikings remained for one year and built large houses, which were taken over by later expeditions. One of these, numbering 160 men and women, stayed on the American continent for three years until they were driven away by Indians.

The truth of these ancient sagas was revealed in 1963–64 by the Norwegian historians and archaeologists Dr. Helge Ingstad and his wife Anne, who after long research which would have been a credit to the most skilled detective, discovered the site of Vinland at L'Anse-aux-Meadows, at the tip of Newfoundland. The explorers unearthed the foundations of Ericsson's houses, one of them seventy feet by fifty-five feet, and various household implements. The date of the finds was established at A.D. 1000 or thereabouts by radio-carbon analysis. This discovery was confirmed by the later finding of a map, drawn in Basel in 1440 from an old monkish manuscript of the twelfth century. This also indicated that the Viking discovery of America had been known to some European scholars for centuries.

Meanwhile, in November, 1002, the English rose against the Danelaw invaders and massacred as many settlers as they could lay hands upon, among them Sven Forkbeard's sister. Egged on by his formidable wife, Sven vowed to conquer all England, and for eleven years his fleets brought axemen and spearmen to ravage the English coasts. At last King Ethelred fled in panic to Normandy and Sven proclaimed himself king of England, only to die a few months later at Gainsborough in Lincolnshire. The Danish army in England chose Sven's son, Canute II, as the successor to the English throne.

OVERLEAF: *An eleventh-century view of a French city under Viking siege.*

Canute returned to Denmark soon after his election, but in 1014 he came back to England with a huge fleet and set about in earnest to conquer the country. In 1016 poor, pious, brokenhearted King Ethelred died in Normandy, and his successor, Edmund Ironside, made a treaty with the 22-year-old Canute, under which England was divided between them. Following tradition, Canute married Emma, Ethelred's widow. Edmund died that same year, leaving the Dane in possession of all England. Two years later when his brother died, Canute formally ascended the throne of Denmark as well, thus becoming the ruler of an Anglo-Scandinavian empire.

We have a picture of King Canute II from one of the Icelandic sagas: "Cnut was of great size and strength and very handsome, except that his nose was thin, high, and slightly bent. He had a light complexion and fair, thick hair, and his eyes surpassed the eyes of most men in their beauty and keenness." Canute proved to be a wise ruler, and, as the ancient chronicler tells us with an understandable note of awe,

"in his kingdom was so good a peace that no one dared to break it."

By now Scandinavia was, nominally at least, Christian. Olaf of Sweden had been baptized in 1008 by an English missionary, which must have infuriated his old pagan mother, and now, in 1027, Canute went on a pilgrimage to Rome, the first Scandinavian monarch to visit the Holy City. The occasion was the coronation of Conrad II as Roman Emperor, and after the ceremony Conrad left Saint Peter's with Canute on his right-hand side, a great lift to Canute's prestige and a proof of the regard in which he was held. As Canute wrote to his English subjects: "I do call you to witness that I have traveled to Rome to pray for the forgiveness of my sins and for the welfare of the peoples under my rule. . . . I have vowed to God to rule my kingdoms justly and piously. . . . Never have I spared—nor shall I spare—to spend myself and my toil on what is needful and good for my people."

Canute founded Denmark's first monastery and built many churches, but he did not feel, in spite of King Olaf's conversion, that Sweden was really Christian. There was still too much worship of the old gods, and so Canute sent English missionaries to the important Swedish trading center of Lund.

The king ordered the missionaries to destroy the community's great idols and when that had been done a swarm of English bishops and priests moved in to complete the work of conversion. Unfortunately, as has happened many times since in the world's history, a lot of second-rate people who had little hope of making a career at home saw in this foreign crusade a splendid chance to make themselves important in a backward country and to live like fighting cocks at the expense of the natives. Many of these missionaries drank themselves to death, and a certain Bishop Henry, it was said, "never raised his hand in blessing unless there was a glass in it."

Meanwhile, another descendant of Harold the Fairhaired, Olaf II, had laid claim to Norway after having served in England. This Olaf is celebrated for having converted Norway to Christianity, a feat he achieved by calling a regional Thing for the purpose of drawing up a church code in 1024. Olaf the Saint, as he was subsequently dubbed, saw to the enactment of severe penalties for those who continued to worship the pagan gods, but he was wise enough to incorporate some of the old ways—the beer feasts for example—into the new liturgy.

This seventh-century bronze plaque depicts two heavily armed warriors.

(Norway's unique stave churches with their fantastic pagoda-like form and dragon carving ornamentation are another indication of the survival of the pagan past long after Olaf's conversion.)

The Norwegian king's efforts on behalf of the Church notwithstanding, he was forced to seek refuge in Sweden in 1028 when Canute sailed to Norway with a fleet of 1,400 ships, won over the people with grand promises, and seized the country in a bloodless campaign. When Olaf tried to recapture Norway two years later, he met death at the Battle of Stiklestad by his own Norwegian peasants. King Canute died in 1035, much mourned in Denmark and in England, and was buried in Winchester Cathedral. His memory is still kept green in both countries, for Canute, "mighty ruler of England, South Scotland, Denmark, Norway, and the Wendish Lands," was one of the first great European statesmen. He was succeeded on the Danish throne by his son, Harthacanute, whose half-brother Harold Harefoot seized the throne of England. Harefoot did not last long, however, for Harthacanute invaded England, killed his half-brother, and threw his body into the Thames. The Dane did not long survive the unlucky Harefoot; Harthacanute died of over-drinking at a wedding feast at Lambeth in 1042. "He never did anything royal," is the laconic estimate of a contemporary chronicler.

The Age of the Vikings was now drawing to a close in a welter of blood. Scandinavia had, through the expansionist drive of its warriors, become a significant participant in the growth of Europe and Christendom. Three distinct, if unsettled, kingdoms had begun to take shape. In Sweden the old royal line, which had ruled from Uppsala, had died out and the country was plunged into civil war. In Norway a ruthless adventurer named Harold Haardraade ("Hard Ruler") seized power and for seventeen years fought the Danish king Sven Estrithson, Sven Forkbeard's grandson, for the Danish throne. Poor embattled Sven was, we are told, "handsome, tall and strong, generous and wise, just and brave but never victorious in war." Nevertheless he did, after years of strife, wear down Harold Haardraade, who finally despaired of getting his hands on Denmark and instead turned his attention to England. Canute the Great's Anglo-Danish empire had fallen to pieces by now and England was ruled by a native prince, Harold II. When Haardraade's Norsemen landed in the north of England, King Harold

King Canute, ruler of Denmark, Norway, and Britain, is shown here with his queen placing a golden cross on the altar of an English church.

hurried to meet them with his Saxon army and at Stamford Bridge utterly defeated the invaders in late September, 1066. Harold Haard-raade died in battle.

Another breed of Norsemen, the Normans, who by now had largely adopted French manners and customs and the French style of warfare, were, in the meanwhile, planning to take advantage of King Harold's absence in the north. The English ruler had no sooner driven the Norwegian invaders into the sea and back to their ships than he was forced to turn southward to meet the Norman threat. Duke William of Normandy, with a large force of cavalry, foot soldiers, and archers, landed near Hastings. The English army, composed for the most part of foot soldiers, marched 150 miles in five days and, as the October dawn broke, King Harold's spearmen and axemen stood ready on the Sussex downs to repel the Normans.

The English failed in the defense of their country. Harold was killed by an arrow and his death so disheartened his troops that they took to their heels, leaving William, henceforward known as the Conqueror, master of England. Two Danish expeditions to recapture the island in 1069 and 1075 had no success, and with their failure the Age of the Vikings ended.

In evaluating the Viking influence on western Europe, it must be concluded that until the middle of the tenth century, at least, the Viking raids were purely destructive, and indeed they nearly brought about the collapse of civilization in western Europe. The ancient culture of Ireland, for example, never recovered from the Norse onslaught. However, the invaders often replaced a ruined and gutted monastery with a trading post which, as time went on, became a city—Dublin and Wexford, for example, are both Viking foundations. Similarly, the Swedes established the cities of Kiev and Novgorod, and the Danes struck firm roots in Normandy, which became, within 150 years of their arrival there, the strongest and most solid principality in western Europe.

From about 950 onward the invaders began to settle in the lands which they occupied and to intermarry with the local population. In England especially this process of assimilation was comparatively easy. The Norsemen who now set about becoming Englishmen, as the Danes in Normandy became Frenchmen, belonged to the same race as the people among whom they lived, and they had certain basic beliefs in common. Chief among these was a respect for law—the very word is derived from a Norse term—and this greatly helped assimilation.

In both England and France the Viking onslaught, disruptive as it was to the cultural life, did at least have the effect of producing local leaders of ability and character who led their people against the invaders and laid the foundations of modern nations in so doing. The Capetian dynasty, which ruled France for so long, was founded by the man who defended Paris against the Danish Vikings, and in England the house of Egbert produced a line of native sovereigns which was only finally extinguished by the Norman Conquest.

The Norman Conquest is one of the landmarks of Western history. The population of England in 1066 was about one and a half million, and Duke William, with no more than 12,000 men, utterly subjugated the country. England, as so often in its later history, had neglected the latest developments in warfare, while the Normans had cultivated them systematically. In particular the English had no understanding, as had the Normans, of the use of cavalry and archers. Never was a country more thoroughly subdued than was England by the Normans, nor more despotically ruled than by these Dano-Frenchmen. Yet the Normans, whom we may call the last of the Vikings, did, for all their tyranny, give England three great blessings—a uniform national code of law, taxes fixed and systematically collected (which is, paradoxically, a blessing), and adequate defense forces loyal to the king rather than to many feudal barons. This was the last, and, perhaps, the greatest achievement of the Norsemen.

CHAPTER II

SCANDINAVIA'S
MIDDLE AGES

T he century that followed the last of the Viking expeditions was
for Scandinavia a time of bloodshed and confusion. In Sweden the
old religion still had many followers—indeed Christianity had not yet
gained any solid foothold there—and for many years the country was
torn apart by bitter warfare between pagans and Christians. English
and German missionaries gradually spread the Gospel, but the old
gods died hard. When, about 1130, a nobleman named Sverker was
elected king and invited monks of the Cistercian order to come to
Sweden and establish monasteries there, many determined animists in
the remoter parts of Sweden still worshiped Thor and Odin; even
the converts, more often than not, regarded Christ as just another god,
rather more powerful than the old deities but otherwise little different
from them.

In Denmark, on the other hand, Christianity was by now firmly
established. Although Sven Estrithson was unlucky in war, he was a
great reformer at home. By the time of his death in 1075, he had
founded six bishoprics, two of them in Skåne, which is now Swedish
but was then a part of Denmark, and hundreds of churches. The Cis-

*The Borgund stave church, begun in 1138, remains one of the finest and best
preserved examples of Norway's unique medieval church architecture.*

tercians had established their order in Denmark in 1150, followed soon after by the other major monastic communities, and through these houses international scholastic and cultural influences were fed into the country. Sven left behind him another memorial—fifteen sons, of whom five became kings of Denmark, and four daughters, all of them illegitimate.

These bastard sons and their offspring plunged Denmark into dynastic warfare which ravaged the country intermittently for eighty years. Finally a young claimant named Valdemar outdistanced two rivals and in 1157 seized the throne. At last victorious, Valdemar ("the Great") found his prize in a dreadful condition. Apart from the ravages of the civil war, about one third of Denmark had been laid waste by the Wends, a branch of the Baltic Slavs which had migrated to the island of Rügen. The new king raised his foster brother Absalon to the bishopric of Roskilde and with this powerful ally set out to subdue the invaders and to unify the divided Danish nation.

For ten years Absalon and the king waged war on the Wendish pirates and at last, in 1169, the Danes captured their island home. The great temple at Arcona and the Wendish capital at Garz were razed to the ground and the many-headed idols of the Slavic gods Svantovit and Rügievit were chopped up to feed the Danish campfires. The Wends were forced to become Christian, whether they liked it or not.

Among the many defensive forts established at this time was a castle built by Absalon at the tiny fishing hamlet of Havn. The fortress, which stood on the site where Christiansborg Palace now stands, became a trading center known as Kaupmanna Havn (Merchants' Haven). The name has come down almost unaltered in Danish as Köbenhavn (Copenhagen).

Valdemar, in a continuing effort to gain control of Denmark and strengthen her international position, had early acknowledged the German emperor Frederick Barbarossa as his overlord, although in the last years of his reign the Dane's remarkable successes against the Wends had encouraged his princes to dabble in the feudal squabbles raging in Germany.

Meanwhile, a modicum of order had also come to the north shores of the Baltic, where trade began to flourish, pirate-infested though the inland sea still was. The keenest merchants were German, a fact which was to influence Scandinavian history for centuries to come. The Germans set up a commercial port within their own territory at Lübeck, and soon their ships swarmed around Gotland, the headquarters of Swedish trade with Russia and the East. The Germans settled in the seaport town of Visby on Gotland Island, and the city soon began to dominate the Baltic. To this day it is one of the notable tourist attractions in Sweden.

Perhaps nowhere in Europe is the spirit of the Middle Ages more alive than in Visby. The rich men of Visby built no fewer than fifteen churches, most of them now in a state of picturesque disrepair, and their trust in God was prudently tempered by a strong mistrust of men. The town is still embraced on three sides by the great wall completed in 1300 behind which the merchants guarded their treasures, and only to seaward is free access given. The walls are studded with watchtowers, from which sentries kept constant vigil. The largest and best preserved of these, the "Powder Tower," affords from its summit a view of a medieval city with which the passing centuries have dealt kindly indeed. The German Hanse, or "Company of Gotland Travelers," competed fiercely with the local merchants for the Russian trade and, reaching across the Baltic, founded the Latvian city of Riga. In 1170 King Canute I of Sweden signed a trade treaty with the Germans, and from that time onward Sweden's maritime power in the Baltic declined.

Rather, Canute concentrated on strengthening Sweden internally. In 1187 pirates from Estonia and Karelia, on the eastern shore of the Baltic, sailed boldly into Lake Mälaren, burned and sacked towns and villages and murdered the archbishop. To prevent such an outrage from happening again Canute built a wooden fort on a small island commanding the entrance to Mälaren. The stronghold was given the name of Stockholm—the future Swedish capital—signifying a stockaded islet.

In 1182 Valdemar I of Denmark died, "lamented," as a chronicler says, "by all Denmark," and was succeeded by his eldest son Canute VI, a pious man who, with the help of the invaluable Absalon, extended Danish dominion over Pomerania and Holstein. By 1184 Canute could style himself "King of the Danes and Wends." On his death in 1202 his brother, Valdemar II ("the Victorious") ascended the throne and reigned for almost forty years. The new king, stirred by still greater ambitions, had made up his mind to extend the Danish sphere of influence eastward and southward into the Baltic and the adjoining German lands. While still a prince he had won control of the chief Baltic seaport of German Lübeck. Now as king he received fealty from a number of German princelings. Estonia, which had harbored so many pirates, was subdued in 1219. The campaign was a bitter one, and it gave rise to one of the great legends of Danish history. In that year, so the story goes, the Danes, in the course of a hard-fought battle near the modern Tallin, lost their banner to the enemy, much to their dismay. The Danish forces were being hard pressed by the heathen and were becoming disheartened when, from the sky, dropped a red flag bearing a white cross. The Danes gained fresh courage from this miracle and, rallying beneath their new standard, defeated the enemy. This magic banner, known as the Dannebrog (Danes' Cloth), was the model for the national flag that has flown over Denmark ever since that day.

Valdemar II, in spite of his proud nickname, was not always lucky. In 1223 he and his eldest son were kidnapped by one of his German vassals while on a hunting expedition and taken to a German prison. With Valdemar out of the way the German lords rebelled and threw off their Danish overlords. Only after two and a half years were Valdemar and his son released, and then on harsh conditions. Except for Rügen and Estonia, Denmark's overseas holdings were no more.

For the rest of his reign Valdemar II devoted himself to reforms at home. Much of his efforts to strengthen and centralize the royal power in Denmark went to nought when his sons fell to warring among themselves. Valdemar in his drive to create foreign markets for Danish agriculture had taxed the land heavily, with the result that many peasants had relinquished land ownership in preference to becoming tenant farmers under the protection of a lord.

When Valdemar died in 1241 Denmark once more fell into chaos. "At the death of Valdemar II," says a monkish historian, "the crown fell off the head of the Danes. From that time forth they became a laughing-stock for all their neighbors through civil wars and mutual destruction, and the lands which they had honorably won were not only lost but caused great disasters to the realm and wasted it." A bad century had begun for Denmark.

Scenes from the Hanseatic port of Visby include a medieval church ruin and the still active Saint Mary's (top left and right) and the city wall (bottom).

Sweden was having better fortune. In 1222 the last king of the old Sverker dynasty died, and was succeeded by Eric Ericsson, a boy of six, later known as Eric XI ("the Lisping and Lame"). But before long the real ruler of Sweden was the king's brother-in-law, Birger Magnusson, who held the important post of Jarl, or earl, of the realm, and was head of Sweden's powerful Folkung family. When in 1250 Eric died, childless, Birger Jarl was in Finland fighting Alexander Nevski's Russian army, and Birger hurried home to find that his 12-year-old son Valdemar had been elected king. Birger as regent took over the government of the country and ruled it well. He crushed all attempts at rebellion, brought in German craftsmen and miners who laid the foundations of Swedish industry, and, by concluding a trade agreement with the Germans in Lübeck, encouraged a great expansion in trade; Stockholm became Sweden's most important city. Birger Jarl also did much to improve the Swedish legal system, usurping the role of lawmaker previously left to conservative provincial Things in order to give the whole of Sweden a basic framework of civil and criminal law.

Until this time the usual method of judging cases both criminal and civil, but especially the former, had been by ordeal. The accused man was thrown into deep water and his guilt or innocence determined by whether he sank or floated, or he was forced to hold a red-hot iron in his hand, and the extent of the damage caused was held to be the indicator of justice in his case. Other forms of ordeal were also employed, but Birger abolished them all and established a system of courts which would be at least recognizable to modern eyes. He also did away with the grosser forms of serfdom, under which the Swedish peasantry suffered, prohibiting individuals from being forced by their poverty into servitude.

Society in Sweden was still primitive. Most Swedes in the Middle Ages lived in small, close-knit villages, surrounded by arable land which was divided into strips among the villagers; beyond lay common pasture and forest. Village life was organized on collective lines, and all the owners of strips sowed and reaped their crops at the same time each year. Each community sought to grow sufficient crops for its own people—trade outside was rare. Their diet was simple—coarse rye bread, turnips, porridge, beer, and sometimes meat and fish. If a man had a large family, however, the amount of land allotted to him was

usually too small to support his brood, and so the younger sons went
to clear the forests and to establish new settlements. Many of these
villages are easily identified today by their names, which end in *torp*
(farm of a settler) or *ryd* (clearing), preceded by the name of the man
who first cleared the ground. Thus the Svenstorps and Gunnarsryds of
Sweden began to sprout along an ever-lengthening frontier. Centuries
later these Svens and Gunnars were to send their descendants across the
Atlantic in the hundreds of thousands, bearing the same pioneering
spirit to the New World.

Many of the great estates of Sweden were owned by the king, the
nobility, or the Church, but they were tilled by freemen under the
supervision of bailiffs. The institution of serfdom, or slavery to put it
more bluntly, was on the decline—by 1335 when it was formally abolished it had all but disappeared in Sweden. Until the rise of Stockholm
the nation's only trading centers of any importance had been Kalmar
and Sigtuna. Gotland, the center of east–west commerce, was an independent community, largely dominated by Germans, who paid tribute
to Sweden in cash and kind but traded for themselves. They maintained
trading posts at Novgorod and Smolensk and shipped their wares to
the German mainland, the Netherlands, and England. Sweden was
something of a backwater.

In Norway life was much harsher. Each isolated settlement, cut off
from its neighbors by fjord, forest, and mountain, struggled grimly to
produce food from the shallow layer of soil, painfully cleared of the
trees and boulders that covered the rocks upon which Norway stands.
In bad years a sort of bread was made from the bark of trees, of which,
at least, there was a plentiful supply, but there was little grazing for
cattle or even for sheep. Fish, fresh, smoked, dried, and salted, was the
foundation of the Norwegian menu, as it is to this day.

During the first half of the twelfth century Norway had been torn
by civil war, for no systematic means of royal succession had been
arrived at. With the accession to the throne in 1162 of Magnus V
Erlingsson an accord was reached with the pope by which the Norwegian king could henceforth be regarded as Saint Olaf's steward and
his rule to exist "by the grace of God." Succession was to be granted
only to those "properly born," that is, the eldest legitimate son. Failing
the existence of such a son, the royal candidate was to be chosen accord-

ing to clearly prescribed legal means. Unlike Sweden and Denmark, where election was the rule, the hereditary principle prevailed in Norway. Norway's dynastic strife seemed to be over.

Meanwhile, events were building toward the union of Norway and Iceland. Settled between the years 870 and 930 by Norsemen from Norway and Celts from what is now Ireland and Scotland, Iceland was ruled by a central parliament, or Althing, the first of its kind in the world. In the year 1000 the Althing officially declared Iceland to be a Christian nation, and over the next 250 years Iceland became a center of culture, if a country so remote can be called a center in any sense.

Early in the thirteenth century, however, civil war broke out among the local chieftains in the colony of Iceland. The pope and King Haakon IV ("The Old") of Norway tried to intervene and at last Haakon resolved to settle the matter by bringing Iceland under Norway's political suzerainty. In return for a guarantee of trade, Iceland recognized the supremacy of the Norwegian crown and Church and agreed to pay taxes. Iceland was, however, allowed to keep its own laws, and the terms agreed upon by King Haakon in 1262 remained the charter of Iceland's liberties until she became a sovereign nation in 1944.

Beginning with Norwegian colonization in the tenth century, the art of heroic poetry flourished in Iceland. The tradition came with the invaders and many of the sagas dwell on ancient Norwegian history, but the poetic gift seems to have been uniquely Icelandic. The earliest works were oral literature, composed by anonymous poets, and they survived from one generation to the next. These and many newly written ones began to be set down on calfskin in the thirteenth century by scholar-monks. Of the vast body of prose and poetry they produced, some seven hundred manuscripts and fragments of manuscripts have survived to inform students of Scandinavian history. The poetry falls into two broad categories—anonymous Eddaic poems, which relate the deeds of ancient pagan gods and mortal heroes, and the scaldic poems, told by professional *skalds,* or poets, and based upon Christian themes and personalities.

The most famous of the historical sagas are, perhaps, the *Hallfreda Saga,* which deals with the days of King Olaf Trygvasson, the *Saga of Eric the Red,* the *Saga of the Greenlanders,* and the *Heimskringla,*

At right is a detail of the princess from "Saint George and the Dragon," a group sculpture carved by Bernt Notke of Lübeck in the fifteenth century.

a collection of sagas written by Snorri Sturleson giving an account of the history of Norway through the semilegendary biographies of its kings, from early times up to the year 1177.

Two collections of sagas exist under the general name of Edda. About the year 1650, after Iceland had become an appendage of Denmark, an Icelandic bishop discovered an old parchment book whose text bore similarities to the known Edda but appeared to be of earlier vintage. He called it the *Elder Edda.* Unhappily for Iceland the bishop's daughter had just been seduced by a young priest, and her angry father was resolved that the girl's honor should be properly avenged. Accordingly he offered his precious manuscripts to the king of Denmark on the strict condition that the erring priest should be heavily punished. We are not told what happened to the poor young man, but in due time the *Elder Edda* found its way to the Royal Library of Copenhagen to the great and lasting resentment of all Icelanders.

In April, 1971, a Danish naval frigate dropped anchor in the harbor of Reykjavík to be greeted by most of the city's seventy thousand inhabitants. The ship brought back, at long last, the precious manuscripts to be given into the care of the Icelandic nation, and the occasion was one of deep rejoicing. For the Icelanders today still hold the world's record as publishers and readers of books. Each year some six hundred new books come off the presses in Reykjavík and most of these run into editions of from five thousand to seven thousand copies. No other nation has so many publishers or readers per capita, although the Finns and Norwegians come close. With this thousand-year tradition of love and respect for the written word, little wonder that the return of their precious sagas meant so much to the people of the little republic.

Meanwhile in Sweden the notable regency of Birger Jarl was coming to an end. In 1266 he died, leaving his son King Valdemar on his own. Valdemar, now aged thirty, set out to prove the well-established fact that the sons of great men rarely live up to the reputation of their fathers. A weak character, entirely given over to pleasure, he immediately quarreled with his younger brother Magnus. In 1275, after years of intermittent strife, Magnus defeated and deposed Valdemar and mounted the throne as "King of the Swedes and the Goths," a title which was now heard for the first time. Magnus I dazzled the simple Swedish folk by the splendor of his court, and he surrounded himself with sophisticated German noblemen. In 1280 the native Swedish nobility, jealous of these foreign interlopers, tried to organize a rising against the king, but it was ruthlessly crushed and its leaders executed.

King Magnus proved a far more worthy son of his father than had his elder brother. Once firmly on the throne he set about developing Sweden's trade and strengthening her links with continental Europe. He continued Birger Jarl's policy of encouraging German craftsmen and miners to settle in Sweden; and from his reign dates the development of the copper mines at Falun and the iron mines in Dalecarlia, Västmanland, and Närke. Magnus was also the founder of Sweden's standing army. By exempting from taxation freemen who were willing, when called upon, to serve under the king's banner, he raised a force of heavy cavalry. These armored horsemen were known as Royal Knights, and to become a member of that body not only kept the tax-man away but conferred much social prestige. In time of war the Royal Knights were required to attach themselves to the bodyguard, or *hird,* of some local nobleman, and thus a class of semiprofessional soldiers was created.

King Magnus can also claim to have founded the Swedish hotel industry. Until his day any nobleman on his travels—and noblemen in the Middle Ages traveled with a large following of retainers, servants, and hangers-on—thought himself entitled to seize food and forage, bed, and any comforts that might go with it from any village in which he chose to spend the night. Magnus put an end to this unpopular custom. He ordained that one householder in each village should place himself at the service of travelers and supply them with shelter, food, and drink, and that he should charge a reasonable price for these amenities. It was forbidden, on pain of severe punishment, to demand such services from any other villager, and the grateful peasants nick-named their king "Ladulås," or Barn Locker, since their stores of food were now safe from highborn plunderers.

To the south, the Danes now took their first real step toward representative government. The king's arbitrary exercise of power, his interference in the functioning of the ancient people's courts, had gone too far. The opposition, led by the growing class of manorial lords, saw in the crown's growing financial crisis a chance to put limits on the king. At Vordingborg, in 1282, Eric V, or Eric Klipping, with the

advice of "the best men of the realm, lay and learned," was compelled to sign a charter, in effect a constitution, defining his duties to the lords. The *Danehof,* or parliament, was in future to be summoned once each year, and it would function as the supreme legislative body of the realm, imprisonment without trial was forbidden, and other reforms, very much on the lines of England's Magna Carta, were introduced. Nevertheless, Eric found means to avoid compliance, and four years later he was assassinated. Encamped after a day of hunting in the countryside, the king was set upon by a band of Danish noblemen and stabbed fifty-six times. Next year his son, Eric Moendved, brought the murderers before a grand jury; nine were found guilty and sentenced to banishment. This punishment, however merciful, was an unfortunate one for Denmark, for the regicides promptly took refuge in Norway, where they found that king only too ready to offer support. For years the assassins, lurking in the islands off the Norwegian coast,

This sheep-shed, built in a centuries-old manner, is located on the Swedish island of Farö, northeast of Gotland in the Baltic Sea.

raided Denmark. The ballads of the time celebrate them as heroes, rather as English rhymsters of roughly the same period glorified the deeds of another outlaw, Robin Hood.

The remainder of Eric Moendved's reign was bedeviled by his brother Christopher, who waged intermittent but unrelenting war against him. When Eric died childless in 1320, Christopher found most of Denmark mortgaged to foreign creditors and the nobility demanding a still larger share of government. Christopher II has been described as "the most faithless and useless ruler Denmark ever had." When he failed to live up to the charter imposed upon him, he was twice driven out of his kingdom, the second time for good, and he died abroad in poverty in 1332.

While Denmark, only recently far more powerful than her northern neighbor, was being partitioned among foreign princes, Sweden embarked upon a short period of greatness. Magnus I died in 1290, and his place on the throne was taken by his eleven-year-old son, Birger. The boy king's mentor and guardian was Marshal Torgils Knutsson, the leader of the royal council, who completed the conquest of Finland, which had been begun by Birger Jarl. Knutsson built a fortress at Vyborg close by a major Russian trade route and, at last, penetrated Russian territory, crossing Lake Ladoga, and traveling as far as Novgorod.

Torgils Knutsson's policy at home was forward-looking and enlightened. Ignoring the fury of the formidable Pope Boniface VIII, Knutsson asserted the power of the State over that of the Church, and he introduced a code of laws which was to have profound effects on the country for centuries to come. The changes were chiefly concerned with land tenure and inheritance and the beginnings of a jury system for criminal trials.

In 1298 Birger came of age and married Princess Märta, sister of King Eric Moendved of Denmark. However, Torgils Knutsson continued to exercise considerable influence: in 1302, the year of Birger's accession to the Swedish throne, Knutsson organized a division of the royal estates inherited from Birger Jarl, with results which were finally fatal to himself. King Birger's younger brother Eric became duke of Södermanland and his second brother, Valdemar, was proclaimed duke of Finland. Since brotherly love does not seem to have

PRO = LO = O

[M]agnus medr guds miskun
regs kongr sun hakonar kong[s]
sunar sun suerris kongs send[ir]
ollum guds vinum ok sinum i
[Gu]la þings loghum. Q. G. ok sine
uitid. at hinir skynsamaztu
i gula þings loghum. hafa id
ga gerd fyrir os at þer hafu
at uer hafum lut latit. at bo
nokkor um flestar leiughbo
i landeno. ok bedit os. at þdu
k skilldi fra umbota eighi l
laus uera. En þer skulut þ
uita sannlegha at os uer adi
fyr at sia. En þo mi einkan
bezt. er þer treystud sua mi
a uara forsio. at þer domit
alla i uara forsio. þat af a
ka. ok þar uid at leggia sem þikkir bezt vera. m; skynsamra
nna rade. Ok þui hafum uer nu um ridit. idulegha skode
na. ok lizt os sem allmikla mætte mædr ferrom ordom þui
oskurd gefua. þar sem hon talade adr gefsi langt um. En
um stodum þyrri hon sannlegha till loghu. þar sem huergin
adr hofare. en margher þyrfte þeir er raunt ir uoro. þui
uer kennum os mioc uankunnende til slikra storuerka þa h[o]
uer þessa bok lated rita er uer sendom yder. treystandi up a u
fra ihc xpc miskun. ok fra hinna skynsamaztu manna tillo[gh]
er hia os uaro. En at þer skilit þui gior hui u hafum so bo
skipat i bokena. sem nu er þa greinir þessir hættir sem her f
þingfarar bolkr er nu sem fyr at anduerdu ritadr fyr e
hefr sealfa bokena. þui at adr ber at skipat se þinget. ok nef

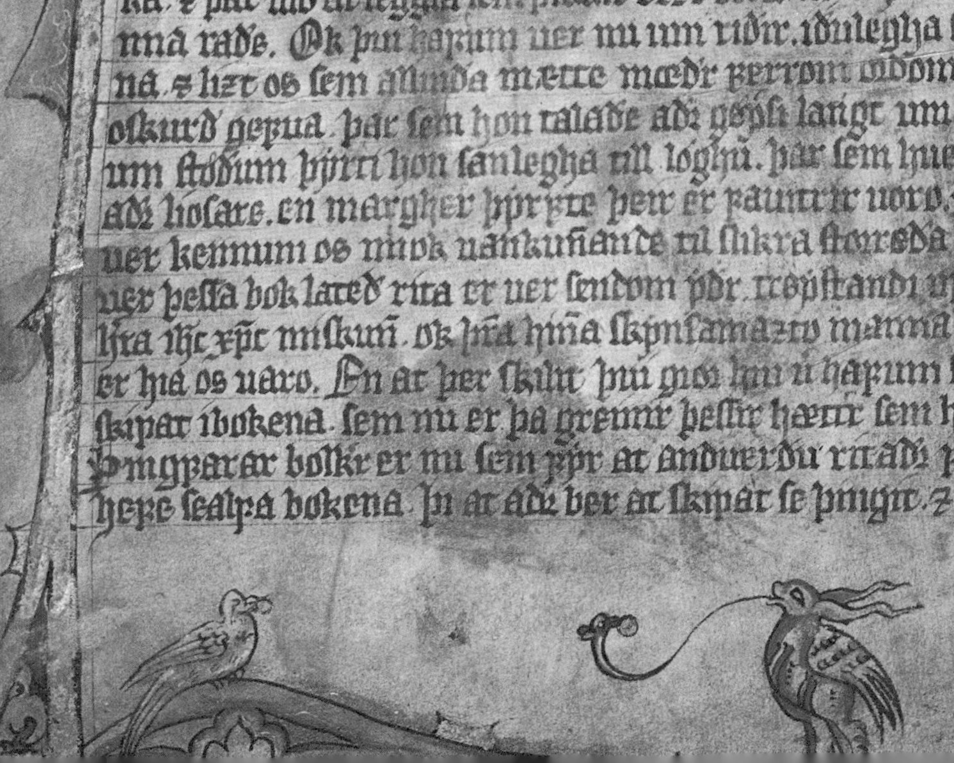

been much practiced in the royal families of Scandinavia, it is hardly surprising that the two dukes lost no time in raising a conspiracy against the king. Defeated, they fled to Norway, whence they sought reconciliation with Birger.

The two dukes tried to persuade the king that all Sweden's troubles were the fault of Torgils Knutsson. Birger, himself irritated by the marshal's autocratic ways, which made him still the real ruler of the country, agreed. In 1306 Knutsson was arrested and brought to Stockholm, where he was publicly beheaded. As the king's guards laid hands on the marshal to arrest him the doomed man cried out: "This will disgrace you everlastingly while you live, O King!"—another of those prophecies which were to prove all too accurate.

Six months had hardly elapsed since Knutsson's execution when King Birger had good cause to regret the trust which he had unwisely placed in his ambitious brothers. Birger had invited the two dukes to a party on the royal farm at Hatuna and all seemed to be going well when the host and his queen were suddenly arrested by their guests and hustled off to prison. This episode, which is known in Swedish history, and rather naturally, as "the Hatuna Surprise," unleashed a civil war.

Getting rid of Birger, however, did not prove all that easy. Thanks to Norwegian and Danish mediation, the king and queen were released after four years and Sweden was divided among the three royal brothers. Birger, however, had not forgotten what had happened at Hatuna; he had to wait another seven years for his revenge. In 1317 the two dukes were invited by the king to a grand banquet at the castle of Nyköping, some fifty miles south of Stockholm. Unable to resist a good dinner, the dukes spent a jolly evening with the king and then went to bed. No doubt there had been a good deal of drink at the feast and the dukes were sleeping soundly when their bedrooms were invaded by Birger and his men-at-arms. If the king had wished to return surprise for surprise he certainly succeeded. The dukes were both wounded, shackled with heavy chains, and thrown into a particularly deep dungeon, where Birger, before locking the door, had much pleasure in reminding them of Hatuna. The king then left his prisoners and threw away the key to their cell, where eventually they both died of starvation.

King Birger soon found that he had to pay heavily for his pleasure.

This manuscript shows Norway's King Magnus, one of the last Viking rulers, as portrayed in a contemporary Bible.

Duke Eric's wife, Ingeborg, daughter of Haakon V of Norway, was not the woman to shrug her shoulders and go on with her embroidery when her husband had been starved to death, and the Swedish nobility, with whom Duke Eric had always been popular, rallied to her side. Birger tried to buy Danish support by offering King Eric Moendved a part of his kingdom, but that monarch, who had plenty of troubles of his own, refused the offer. Norway naturally supported their own princess and sent troops to join her forces. The rebels took the field against the king in such strength that Birger, sure that his cause was lost, fled to Gotland, leaving behind his son and his chief adviser, both of whom were immediately executed. Birger took refuge in Denmark and died there in 1321. He lies now at Ringsted, the only Swedish king to be buried on Danish soil.

Duke Eric's son, Magnus, was only three when he was elected king of Sweden in 1319. In the same year the child's grandfather King Haakon died and little Magnus Ericsson succeeded him as king of Norway. Thus Sweden and Norway were nominally united under a single king, but the union was a purely formal one, and everyone presumed it would last only during the life of the king.

When King Magnus Ericsson came of age in 1332 Sweden was more prosperous and powerful than she had ever been, but Denmark was in the last stages of collapse. Eric Menved had died in 1319 and the feckless Christopher was powerless to maintain control. The fertile region of Skåne was then a part of Denmark, although it was ruled by the German count of Holstein. In 1332 the Skanian peasants rose in revolt against their German masters and the count was happy to sell Skåne and the province of Blekinge to King Magnus for a large sum of money. Eight years later Christopher's son became the new king of Denmark as Valdemar IV Atterdag. He confirmed this sale and added to it the province of Halland, on the west coast of Sweden, in return for 50,000 silver marks or, say, $8,500,000 in today's money.

King Valdemar IV Atterdag proved a more clever and effective ruler than his father. When he came to the throne in 1340 the fortunes of Denmark were at their lowest ebb. All but a single county in Jutland was under foreign rule and the young king—he was twenty years old at his accession—had to scrape along with only the revenues of that tiny enclave to support him. Magnus' Swedish silver was therefore

very welcome and Valdemar used it well. By 1349 Valdemar had
driven the foreigners from a great part of Denmark.

However, another kind of adversary threatened. Scandinavia fell victim to an invasion from England which brought death to many thousands of people. The bubonic plague, or Black Death, had come to Europe from the Levant, brought by infected rats from the holds of merchant ships. This horror was already ravaging the Continent and England when, in 1349, so the story goes, an English merchantman with a cargo of wool put into the Norwegian port of Bergen. "Put in" is perhaps not the right term to use, since the ship had no crew except rats. Every man had died on the voyage of the dreadful sickness, and when the ship drifted ashore on the Norwegian coast the rats scuttled to land and Bergen was soon in the grip of the plague.

The epidemic quickly spread to Trondheim, where it killed the archbishop and every member of his chapter but one, and in an incredibly short space of time the pestilence had spread to the whole of Norway and killed off two thirds of its people. The plague came to Sweden in 1350 and found King Magnus no better equipped to deal with it than any other European monarch. The king declared in a proclamation, "God, for the sins of the world, has struck the world with this great punishment of sudden death. By it most of the people in the land to the west of our country are dead. It is now ravaging Norway and Halland and is approaching our Kingdom of Sweden."

The remedies which the king ordained in this proclamation were that his subjects should eat nothing on Fridays but bread and water or bread and ale, they were to walk barefoot to their parish churches, and carry holy relics around their cemeteries. These measures, obviously, did little to halt the infection, which killed many thousands of Swedes.

Quite apart from the plague, King Magnus had a load of other troubles to bear. His large but sparsely populated kingdom was extremely difficult to manage. His principal concern was with Sweden, and, in consequence, Norway was left with almost no government at all. Until the Black Death undermined their efforts, Magnus' Norwegian subjects made several attempts to throw off his rule and elect a king of their own. Moreover Valdemar Atterdag, having safely pocketed Magnus' money for the sale of Denmark's southern Swedish

OVERLEAF: *The survival of pagan belief is suggested in this medieval tapestry showing priests ringing church bells to frighten evil spirits.*

holdings, was now scheming to regain the territory. To make things still worse, the Swedish treasury was empty, and as a measure of economy the king cut back the exemption from taxation granted to the Church and the nobility, thus making enemies of both.

In particular Magnus provoked a lady named Birgitta, daughter of a family of powerful nobles, who had been one of the brighter ornaments of his court. When her husband died after a pilgrimage to Santiago de Compostela in Spain, she began to have visions of Christ and the Virgin and to record her experiences in a remarkable work entitled *Revelations*. On the advice of heavenly voices, the prophet warned Magnus against Valdemar (quite rightly), and led the Church's opposition to the king's taxation measures.

This busy woman also founded the Order of the Saviour or Brigittine—whose houses were to become major centers of pietistic and intellectual activity throughout medieval Scandinavia. Enlisting the support of Magnus, who donated the royal estate of Vadstena for the site of her first convent, she then went to Rome to gain the papal blessing. But a schism in the Catholic Church and the unorthodoxy of her proposal delayed approval for some twenty years. Undaunted, she finally achieved her goal in 1367. She died in Rome six years later, just after returning from a pilgrimage to the Holy Land, and it was her daughter, Catherine, who completed the work at Vadstena. The order, which took in both men and women, spread rapidly after Birgitta's death, numbering at one time more than eighty houses throughout Europe. She was canonized in 1391 and chosen as patron saint of Sweden.

In 1360 Birgitta's warnings against the perfidy of Valdemar Atterdag of Denmark were amply justified. In an attempt to keep his kingdom together Magnus had transferred Skåne to his son Eric XII. When Eric died of the plague (or, as some say, of poison) in 1359, Valdemar seized the opportunity to invade Skåne with a large army and open negotiations with Magnus. These ended with the cession of Skåne, which was to remain Danish for the next three hundred years. In the following year Valdemar captured the Hanse-held island of Gotland and seized the vast stores of treasure in Visby. This inevitably led to war between Denmark and Valdemar's one-time supporters, the Hanseatic League.

The League was now at the very height of its power. It held a virtual stranglehold on Scandinavian trade and was instrumental in putting a number of Scandinavian kings on their thrones, Valdemar among them. It will be remembered that German traders had begun to compete with native traders back in the twelfth century. By 1163 the Germans settled in Gotland were sufficiently numerous to be granted the right to run their own community according to their own laws. From this grew a local association, or *"hanse,"* for mutual protection. Similarly, independent hanses were forming in London, in Novgorod, in Bruges, and in Bergen, and upon the privileges granted these enclaves was based the later structure of the confederation or League of Hanse Cities. A commercial treaty between Hamburg and Lübeck in 1241 is generally taken as the first instance of league cooperation and by the end of the century seventeen other Hanse cities had been brought into the system.

By Valdemar's time, the League had developed its own fleet, army, and police force, although its preferred method of handling disputes was through economic sanctions. Its headquarters were at Lübeck, where delegates from seventy towns and cities met at an annual *diet,* or convention.

The Hanse operated what would now be called a "protection racket" on an enormous scale. Woe betide the city or the individual merchant who defied the strict rules of the League or refused to join it if pressed to do so. Rebels were squeezed out of business remorselessly and private traders who tried to operate on the fringes of the League in the hope of picking up a few crumbs of its prosperity were heavily taxed and forced to pay crippling tolls. Even a proud city such as Brunswick was humbled by the merchant princes of Lübeck. The city was expelled from the League for a breach of its rules, and thereafter systematically ruined. The burgomasters of other towns that had offended the Hanse were forced, as the price of forgiveness, to walk barefoot through the streets of Lübeck at the annual convention, wearing penitent robes and carrying candles, while the mob jeered and pelted them with garbage.

It was not easy for an individual to become a member of the Hanse. The League could afford to be selective, since hundreds of young businessmen were eager to share the privileges of membership. Most applicants were rejected out of hand, but those who were chosen as possible members were subjected to initiation rites which were devised to deter all but the most resolute candidates.

The would-be member was, in the first place, forced to take a vow of celibacy for the next ten years, since the Hanse, which had a highly developed sense of secrecy, was not prepared to risk the telling of professional secrets in the bedroom. The initiation ceremony then began. We have an account of one of these affairs from Bergen, a Norwegian seaport in which the Hanse was virtually the sole ruler. When the time for the ceremony came around, the city made a festival of the occasion. The streets were filled with hucksters, sideshows, and beggars, and the people prepared for several days of merriment. Not so the candidates.

For some days before the ceremony officials of the Hanse had arranged for the collection of a large load of excrement, garbage, putrid fish, and old horsehair. This unappetizing mess was brought to one of the huge Hanse "factories" at dockside, piled into a large fireplace, and lighted. Then the candidates' ordeal began: they were first dangled in harnesses above the fire to be choked by the nauseous smoke and half roasted by the heat. Every now and then they were lowered to the ground and put through a barrage of questions, which they were expected to answer intelligently. The applicants who survived this were then given a banquet, where they were forced to eat until they were almost at bursting point. They were then stripped naked and towed out to sea in an open boat, from which they were thrown three times into the water and whipped each time they rose to the surface, the purpose of this test, according to the Hanse, being to prove that the candidates were indeed men and not women.

Finally the young men who had stood up to all these rigors had to face the last and final torture. The candidates marched in procession into the League's Great Hall, where stood an altar and tables laid for a plentiful feast. They were forced to listen to a long moral lecture before sitting down to an enormous meal at which care was taken that they should be hopelessly drunk before the end. Then to a clash of cymbals each man was laid upon the altar and whipped with long, supple rods until his back was flayed. This beating often resulted in death, but those who remained alive after it were given a second ban-

Escutcheon of a Nov-
gorod pilot which once
adorned a Hanse factory

quet and a second whipping for good measure. The survivors were then admitted to membership in the Hanse.

The guests at these exhibitions seem to have enjoyed them very much. King Christian IV of Denmark and Norway, who attended one much later when the Hanse was in decline, recorded his pleasure at the occasion and noted with satisfaction that every window in the hall was broken by the revelers, which seems to have been proof of a thoroughly good party.

In fairness to the Hanseatic League, however, it should be said that, rough though their methods may have been, its members rendered great services to commerce in a turbulent age. If any member of the League was convicted of selling goods of inferior quality he was expelled and ruined. Pirates feared to attack Hanse ships, well knowing that a terrible revenge would follow if they did, and the League's police ensured that the main roads of northern Europe were kept in reasonable repair and that highway robbers got short shrift.

It was this powerful organization which Valdemar of Denmark challenged when he occupied Gotland. The Hanse fleet put to sea to crush the Danish interlopers and was smartly defeated by Valdemar in an action off Hälsingborg, in Skåne, in 1362. The Hanse then entered into an alliance with King Magnus of Sweden and his son Haakon, who had been installed by his father as puppet king of Norway to keep the fractious Norwegians quiet. The purpose of the alliance was to smash Denmark, but it soon ran into difficulties. Young Haakon decided that he would make a better king of Sweden than his father; in this ambition he was encouraged by the tireless Birgitta and most of the Swedish nobility, who had never forgiven Magnus for reducing the tax concessions allowed the Church and the aristocracy. Magnus' loss of Skåne now gave them an additional grievance.

The rebels recognized Haakon as king of Sweden, but this did not greatly help him, because another candidate for the honor was now pushed onto the stage. Duke Albert of Mecklenburg had married the sister of King Magnus and he proposed that his son, also Albert, should be Sweden's king. The Hanseatic League and the nobles, motivated by narrow class interests, quickly switched their allegiance to the wily Albert; Magnus and Haakon, their quarrel hastily patched up if not forgotten, entered into alliance with Valdemar Atterdag of Denmark,

the agreement sealed by Haakon's marriage to Valdemar's daughter
Margaret. Magnus and his son assembled an army in Norway, but were decisively beaten in 1365, and Magnus was taken prisoner. After a good deal of bargaining Magnus recognized Albert as king of Sweden and was released in 1371. Three years later the ex-king was drowned in a storm at sea and the Swedes, who had nicknamed him "Smek" (Pansy), did not lament him.

The 1365 defeat of Valdemar Atterdag's allies did not, however, resolve the struggle between Denmark and the Hanseatic League. A truce was agreed upon, but when Valdemar continued to disturb Hanse trade, representatives met and made preparations once again to go to war. On learning of this new turn, Valdemar went off in search of military assistance, leaving Denmark in a vulnerable state. The Hanseatic fleet delivered a decisive blow to Valdemar's army in 1369, seized Skåne, and entered negotiations with the Danish Council. In 1370, the resulting peace of Stralsund secured for the Hanse complete freedom of trade in Denmark, a host of extraterritorial privileges, and the authority to ratify all future candidates to the Danish throne. To guarantee that the terms would be honored, the Hanse was to hold four strategic fortresses in Skåne and collect two thirds of the revenue of the region for fifteen years. Valdemar Atterdag's humiliation was too much for him and he died five years later.

Thus ended the first brief union of Sweden and Norway. Haakon VI remained king of Norway; his wife Margaret was now preparing to write her own chapter in Scandinavian history.

CHAPTER III

ROYAL UNION, PEASANT SEPARATISM

Albert of Mecklenburg, as king of Sweden, and his foreign regime never had a hope of being effective. The real government of the country, if one can speak of government at this time, was in the hands of the chief "Councilor of the realm," a gangster-like figure named Bo Jonsson Grip, who made the whole of Finland and most of Sweden his personal property. This was a black time for the farmers and peasants, since the noblemen, with nothing to restrain them, plundered the countryside and murdered its inhabitants at will. Sweden's old Folkung dynasty (which dated from Birger Jarl's regency) was temporarily eclipsed, waiting only for a chance to return to power. Most Swedes, resenting their German overlords, heartily wished that it might be so. In 1375 Valdemar IV Atterdag of Denmark died, and five years later his son-in-law Haakon VI, king of Norway and son of Magnus of Sweden, followed him to the grave. In the meanwhile Haakon's queen, Margaret, had managed to have her son Olaf elected king of Denmark in 1376; on Haakon's death Olaf also inherited the crown of Norway, with his mother as regent of both kingdoms.

It was only a matter of time before Margaret, as the effective ruler

Sweden's Kalmar Castle, built in the twelfth century, was a long-time royal residence and important stronghold in the long wars with Denmark.

of both Denmark and Norway, would attack Sweden. In 1386 that time had come; the rapacious Bo Jonsson Grip died and Albert of Mecklenburg, in a belated attempt to exert his authority, tried to seize Grip's vast estates and to subdue the disorderly Swedish nobility. They appealed to Margaret for help, offering the crown of Sweden to Olaf in return for her support against the German oppressors. In 1387, however, Olaf died (allegedly from poison) and the Folkung dynasty was extinct.

Margaret did not allow this misfortune to interfere with her plans, and she continued to rule Denmark and Norway. In 1388 she made a pact with the Swedish nobles, who agreed that she should become regent of Sweden also if she would help them drive Albert from the throne. A year later Margaret's Danish and Norwegian forces invaded Sweden, where they were joined by the rebellious Swedish aristocrats and their followers. Albert mustered what troops he could to meet the invaders and the two armies joined battle near Falköping, in south-central Sweden. Albert and his supporters, many of whom were Germans, mostly Mecklenburgers like himself, were soundly beaten and Albert, his son, and many German knights in his service were made prisoners.

Soon Margaret held all Sweden, with the exception of Stockholm, where the German garrison held out grimly, disposing of Margaret's Swedish supporters by murdering them and burning down their houses.

Nevertheless Margaret was now "Our Sovereign Lady of Sweden." For a time Sweden and Denmark were without a king of their own and Margaret also ruled them directly, but Norwegian law required the election of a monarch, and Margaret chose young Eric of Pomerania, the grandson of her sister and already king of Norway, for the job. Denmark, Norway, and Sweden were at last brought under a unified leadership, and a new phase in their history had begun.

Stockholm, which was still held by Germans, became a center of piracy, offering shelter to members of a German outlaw gang who called themselves "Vitalians," an allusion to their alleged activities as victualers to the city when it was under siege. These marauders, who also established Baltic bases at Rostock and Wismar in Germany, brought Scandinavian commerce almost to a standstill, and Margaret, in alliance with the Hanse, whose trade had suffered heavily from the pirates, set herself to exterminate the sea robbers. Margaret had one important asset in the person of the former King Albert, who was still her prisoner, and she used him as a bargaining counter in her parleys with the Stockholm garrison. At last in 1395 it was agreed that in return for Albert's freedom Stockholm should be handed over to the Hanseatic League for a period of three years, after which it would be given to Margaret, unless Albert could raise ransom of sixty thousand silver marks. When Albert failed to meet the demand, the Hanse moved into Stockholm and the Vitalians hastily took refuge in their other bases. For the next three years Swedish and Hanseatic warships hunted down the pirates relentlessly and at last utterly destroyed them.

With Stockholm safe in more or less friendly hands Margaret was free to act. This first great exponent of Scandinavian union set in motion her plan to consolidate the three kingdoms of which she was the regent. In 1396 Norway's King Eric was proclaimed king of Denmark and Sweden also, and in the same year the Swedish nobility undertook to surrender to Margaret all crown lands which they had misappropriated during the past thirty-three years in Albert's lawless reign and to demolish all fortresses and castles built during that time. Margaret also sought to rebuild the financial health of the crown. She demanded the restoration of taxes on all the nobility's estates—many of which had been exempted by Albert in his efforts to gain support— and the noblemen accepted Margaret's dictum with hardly a word of protest.

Then, on June 17, 1397, the leaders of Denmark, Norway, and Sweden gathered in southeast Sweden, at Kalmar, whose great castle still glowers down on the Baltic Sea. Eric of Pomerania was crowned king of Norway, Sweden, and Denmark, in the grandest ceremony Scandinavia had ever seen. The Union of Kalmar, it was proclaimed, should bring the three kingdoms "eternal and unbroken peace." State councils, drawn from the best qualified men in each nation, would advise the king, and each realm within the federation would retain its own laws and privileges and only native-born citizens would be eligible for public office. This latter stipulation seems to have been ignored by Margaret, who was a Dane by birth. Her authority in Sweden and Norway continued to be strong, probably because nobody could pluck up the courage to enforce the eligibility rule.

Margaret's subjects can hardly be blamed for their timidity, for Margaret was one of the great women of all history, worthy to rank with Elizabeth I of England and Catherine the Great of Russia. She now ruled over the largest territory in Europe, but the combined populations of the three kingdoms totaled only one and a half million, of whom half were Margaret's Danish countrymen. Denmark, therefore, took the lead in the union and the regent came to look upon Sweden and Norway as mere appendages of little consequence in the ordering of royal priorities. This attitude did not bode well for the newly established union, and from the outset this shaky federation ran into trouble.

Margaret did, however, provide her subjects with strong government, which, particularly in Sweden, had long been lacking. Although the Swedes were heavily taxed and were mortified to see most of their money spent in the interests of Denmark, they forgave Margaret much, for she had a strong sense of what would now be called "public relations" and an understanding of her subjects' feelings. A brilliant example of this woman's subtle effectiveness was exhibited in the support she gave to the canonization of Saint Birgitta and her visits to the Brigittine monastery at Vadstena. On one of these occasions, in 1403, Margaret asked to be admitted to the community as a sister and this was granted. As the queen was about to leave the monastery all the communicants were lined up and the new sister kissed the hand of each. It is recounted that one bashful lay brother, feeling his flesh unworthy of meeting the royal lips, wrapped his hand in his cloak before holding it out to the queen and was soundly rebuked for his "false humility."

However, Eric, the nominal ruler of the union, was a great trial to the regent. The young man was rash, violent, and obstinate, and in 1410 he managed to involve the nations over which he was supposed to rule in a long and costly war with the duchy of Holstein, which lies on the southern border of Denmark. Margaret had done all she could to avoid the war, and now she tried to mediate between Eric and Gerhard, the duke of Holstein. She was by now in her sixtieth year, an old woman as age went in those days, and she had lived an exacting life. She died in October, 1413, while trying to bring the war to an end. The union which she had established began to break up at once.

Margaret's humanity and her hatred of the war into which Eric had dragged the union was displayed in her last testament. The queen

A Danish medieval drinking vessel, fashioned out of hollowed horn

named as beneficiaries many of her subjects who had suffered humiliation or loss in the Holstein war, and she left money to pay for Masses to be said for the souls of everyone who had been killed in the conflict, no matter what their allegiance.

The war with Holstein continued to drag on and King Eric was so taken up with it that he had no time to visit his Swedish dominions or to attend to their affairs. The enforcement of decisions concerning Sweden were left to royal bailiffs, who in spite of the eligibility clause were mostly Danes or Germans. The Swedish people were ground down by the heavy taxes extorted to finance the king's war, and their plight became extreme when, in 1426, Eric contrived to add the Hanse to his enemies. The League blockaded the coast of Sweden and, since all Swedish trade passed through its hands in normal times, the country's commerce and industry were speedily brought to ruin.

Driven to the last stages of desperation, Sweden was saved by the appearance of a man whom historians were to celebrate as "the champion of Swedish liberty" and "the greatest of medieval Swedes." Engelbrekt Engelbrektsson came of a family of German miners, who had come to Sweden and settled in Dalecarlia northwest of Stockholm

more than a century earlier. The German miners who had made their homes in Sweden under the policies of enlightened immigration pursued by Birger Jarl and Magnus I were by now a privileged class, their status well above that of their peasant neighbors. Some of them, including Engelbrekt's family, were regarded as minor gentry and had become leaders in their districts.

Engelbrekt, as a local man of influence, fell foul of a royal bailiff, a Dane named Jens Ericsson, notorious for his brutal treatment of the peasants. He had an unpleasant habit of seizing the horses of farmers in payment for overdue taxes and of forcing their former owners to drag the plow and their wives and children to be harnessed to the farm carts. At last Engelbrekt himself went to Denmark to lay a complaint against Ericsson before the king. Eric told his Swedish Council to look into the matter, but although they proved that all Engelbrekt's charges were true the bailiff was allowed to continue his reign of terror unchecked.

Once again Engelbrekt traveled to Denmark and protested and this time King Eric lost his temper. "Do not come before my eyes again with your continual complaints!" the king cried, to which Engelbrekt retorted, menacingly: "I shall come back once more, but only once." He returned to Dalecarlia and stumped the country, speaking with a simple eloquence to large gatherings of peasants and miners. In 1434 the Dalecarlians rose in revolt and, under Engelbrekt's leadership, marched through the provinces of Västmanland and Uppland toward Vadstena, where the council was sitting, adding recruits on the way.

The council had been ordered by King Eric to negotiate with the rebels, but Engelbrekt had had more than enough of the king's temporizing. When he reached Vadstena at the head of a formidable force of countryfolk, armed with scythes, flails, pitchforks, and whatever other weapons they could collect, the peasant leader demanded that the councilors join him in deposing the king. At first they refused, but they began to reconsider when Engelbrekt threatened to hand them over to the infuriated peasants for summary execution; to emphasize his demand, he gripped several dignified gentlemen by the throat and half throttled them. Thus encouraged to do what they were told, the councilors obediently signed articles declaring that Eric was no longer king of Sweden.

Engelbrekt, intent on ridding Sweden of the foreigners, then divided
his forces into three offensive columns. Castle after castle fell to the
rustic soldiers, who were joined by many eager helpers as they marched
along. Engelbrekt himself led a force southwestward and occupied the
coastal province of Halland, from which position he could intercept
traffic in the Kattegat and, thus, passage to Danish Jutland, Norway,
and the North Sea. News now reached him, however, that the king
had set sail from Copenhagen to Stockholm, one of the few fortresses
still in his possession, and wished to negotiate in person. The outcome
of the haggling which followed was that Engelbrekt unwillingly consented to place the quarrel between the king and his subjects before
an international tribunal. But since the peasant leader knew that this
court would be heavily loaded in favor of King Eric, he decided to call
his own revolutionary assembly. This gathering, the first *Riksdag,* or
popular parliament, in Swedish history, met at the town of Arboga,
some seventy-five miles west of Stockholm, in January, 1435. It accepted the revolutionary principle, laid down by Engelbrekt, that all
subjects of the king had the right as well as the duty to uphold law
and order and it elected Engelbrekt regent of Sweden.

The Union, as it had been formed by Margaret, was thus broken,
and the representatives of the Swedish nobility, who still favored
union, albeit one more responsive to Swedish interests, tried anew to
restore it. They suggested that the king should retain only ceremonial
power, giving up all real authority to a council, which would be the
permanent government of the country. No foreign bailiffs would be
allowed to operate in Sweden and castles and fortresses would be under
the command of Swedish officers only. Engelbrekt, who was resolved
to destroy the union under which Sweden had been so sadly neglected
and misgoverned, nevertheless agreed to these terms in order to avoid
civil war.

King Eric, however, procrastinated for a year, and in January,
1436, Engelbrekt called a second Riksdag in Arboga and this body
sent Eric an ultimatum. The king did not reply. Thereupon the assembly, fearing that Engelbrekt might, if given his head, become a tyrant,
instituted a joint regency. Karl Knutsson, a descendant of Torgils
Knutsson, who had effectively ruled Sweden almost a century and a
half earlier and whose family had been influential in Swedish affairs

for a much longer period, was elected coregent to check the impetuous temperament of the peasant leader. Eric was then promptly deposed in fact, if not yet in law, and within a few weeks Engelbrekt was murdered at Örebro, near Arboga, by the son of a state councilor loyal to the fallen king. Engelbrekt was buried in Örebro Church, which soon became a goal of pilgrims, many of whom honored the martyred leader as a saint. In his extraordinary political career, which lasted for only three years, Engelbrekt could show great achievements. He had revived the political power of the peasant class, created a representative national assembly, upheld the independence of Sweden, and smashed Margaret's Scandinavian Union. In the words of a German chronicler of the time: "He was chosen by the Lord and endowed with power like Saul to defend his people, and to lay low the adversaries of Righteousness. Engelbrekt surely did not begin this war from any pride of the spirit or from lust of power, but from compassion for those who were downtrodden."

Karl Knutsson, who now became sole regent of Sweden, for the first time assumed the title *Riksförestandare,* or "Leader of the Realm," and his rule was harsh. The peasants, having been made conscious of their power by Engelbrekt, made several attempts to rise against the regent, but these scattered revolts were suppressed. Meanwhile, Eric remained nominal king of Sweden—his formal deposition would not take place until 1439. He was also king of Denmark and Norway but, perhaps wisely, he preferred not to venture into either of those countries. Instead he took refuge with his favorite mistress on the island of Gotland. For the next ten years he lived by piracy, harassing Scandinavian shipping until he was driven out in 1449 by the Swedes, who handed Gotland over to the Danes. Eric retired to his native Pomerania, where he died in 1459.

Denmark was the first of the three kingdoms to set about restoring the old order. In 1439 the Danes elected Christopher of Bavaria, Eric's nephew, as their king, and this was followed by his election to the throne of Sweden in 1440 and of Norway in 1442. The Union was thus temporarily revived. The short reign of Christoper III was not a happy one. When his council complained that Eric's piratical raids were doing great damage to trade, the king's only answer was that his uncle was also entitled to make a living as best he could. The Danish

Herds of reindeer such as this have traditionally provided the Lapps of Norway and Finland with a source of food and skins for tents and clothing.

peasants, reduced to starvation, several times tried to remedy their grievances by force and each time were brutally repressed by the king, to whom they gave the unflattering nickname "the Bark King," since they were driven in their extremity to make bread from tree bark.

When Christopher died, unmourned and without an heir, in January, 1448, Count Christian of Oldenburg, another German, was elected king of Denmark, and the Danish Council called for a meeting of leaders of the three countries of the Union to elect him king of Sweden and Norway also. But Karl Knutsson, having tasted power and eager to regain it at the first opportunity, had been biding his time in Finland, and he now appeared before Stockholm with a sizeable army. The city welcomed him in May, 1448, and he was crowned king of Sweden at Uppsala soon afterward.

The "eternal and unbroken peace" stipulated by Margaret's Union of Kalmar had lasted just fifty-one years. Now war broke out between Denmark and Sweden, and the Norwegians sided with the Swedes, whom they looked upon as less oppressive rulers than the Danes. Knutsson was elected king of Norway in 1449, but the election was hotly opposed by the Swedish nobility, who continued to support the original concept of the Union. At a private peace conference held without Knutsson's knowledge, the Swedish and Danish noblemen declared on their own authority that Knutsson had renounced the crown of Norway in favor of Christian I of Denmark and that the full union would be restored on the death of either Knutsson or Christian. Knowing how unpopular he was with the Swedish peasantry, Knutsson did not dare defy this edict and he abdicated the Norwegian crown. But Christian then made such heavy demands of territory on Sweden that the war was resumed. Knutsson discovered and foiled a plot against his life. The struggle dragged on for another six years.

At last, in 1457, Archbishop John Oxenstierna appeared at Uppsala Cathedral clad in full armor. Laying his crosier upon the high altar, the archbishop vowed that he would not carry it again "until all was changed in Sweden." The militant archbishop, with the support of the unionist noblemen, organized a surprise attack on Knutsson. He fled to the Hanse stronghold of Danzig and the archbishop, together with Eric Tott, a Danish nobleman, took over the reins of government. The Swedish aristocracy, knowing that they now held the whip hand, forced

This statue depicts the Swedish liberator Engelbrekt Engelbrektsson, who led a peasants' rebellion in Dalecarlia in 1434.

Christian to agree to large concessions as a condition of becoming king of Sweden, and, after Christian's coronation, the nobles proceeded to slice up Sweden among themselves.

In 1460, Christian, smarting under the arrogance of the Swedish nobility, took advantage of the death of the duke of Holstein to restore his prestige by gaining control of that neighboring duchy. With heavy bribes, which he financed through tax levies, Christian managed to be elected duke. He also tried to establish his dynasty as Sweden's hereditary royal family by naming his three-year-old son John as heir.

Archbishop Oxenstierna had by now put away his armor and taken up the crosier once more, and it was to him that the peasants of Uppland, brought to beggary by Christian's taxation, appealed for relief in 1463. The archbishop granted their requests only to find himself imprisoned and carried off to Denmark by the infuriated monarch. The king's troops then descended upon Uppland and put hundreds of countryfolk to the sword.

The savage revenge lost Christian any sympathy which the Swedish nobility may still have had for him. In January, 1464, the archbishop's supporters rose in revolt. Their leader was the bishop of Linköping, Kettil Vasa, who came of a family soon to become famous in Sweden and in the world. Many of Karl Knutsson's followers joined the disillusioned Unionists under the inspiration of Knutsson's nephew, Sten Sture, who rallied the peasants to his banner. Although Christian brought reinforcements from Denmark, he failed to crush the rebellion and was obliged to withdraw to lick his wounds and to gather fresh forces. Sture, however, exacted a price from the aristocracy for his support, without which Christian could not have been defeated. The nephew forced them to recall Karl Knutsson to the throne. He came back in 1464, but his power was almost nil, and he was used by Bishop Vasa as a lever to secure the return of Archbishop Oxenstierna to his see. No sooner had the warlike prelate once more set foot on Swedish soil than he began to organize a plot against Knutsson, and in 1465 Knutsson was again forced to abdicate and take refuge in Finland.

Archbishop Oxenstierna now began to bargain with Christian for his return to Sweden, naturally on terms highly favorable to the nobility. The nobles, however, were far from united among themselves and some of them conspired with Knutsson. Eric Tott, who had once been coregent with the archbishop, again proclaimed himself regent and war broke out with Denmark. This time Oxenstierna was on Christian's side, and when the Danish army was defeated near Stockholm in 1467 the archbishop escaped to Denmark, where he soon died.

Now Karl Knutsson was recalled to the throne for the third time. Although he was by no means a great man and suffered throughout his political life from his inability to win the love and trust of the peasants, as Engelbrekt had done, Knutsson has a place of honor in the story of Sweden; in his time he provided a focal point for Swedish dreams of freedom and independence. Before he died in May, 1470, Knutsson named Sten Sture as succeeding regent. Sture was never to seek the title of king and thus initiated the period which has come to be known as "the Sture Age."

Christian, of course, was far from being reconciled to the turn of events in Sweden, and in the summer of 1471 his fleet set sail for Stockholm carrying with it a large and well-equipped army. Upon landing in Sweden the Danish forces were joined by the Unionist nobility, and the combined armies laid siege to Stockholm. Sture called upon the peasants of Svealand, the great province that stretches almost from the Baltic to the Norwegian frontier, to rally to the Swedish cause, and they came in the thousands. The rustic Swedish army then marched upon Stockholm, and on October 10, 1471, one of the great dates of Swedish history, they confronted the Danes on the heights of Brunkeberg, just beyond the northern wall of the city.

The battle that followed ended in a complete triumph for Sture's legions. The *Dannebrog*, that miraculous standard, was captured by the embattled countryfolk, Christian himself was wounded, and the flower of Danish nobility was killed. This decisive victory gave Sweden peace with Denmark for a generation, and in thankfulness for the country's deliverance Sten Sture commissioned the German wood carver Bernt Notke to fashion a heroic statue of Saint George, the city's patron saint. The statue was presented to Sture in the Church of Saint Nicholas, in Stockholm. It stands there to this day, gloriously ornate: Saint George, in splendid armor, his horse similarly caparisoned and plumed, rides with sword raised, while beneath the hoofs of his rearing steed writhes a dragon of singularly repellent aspect.

Christian, his military ambitions considerably reduced, now set him-

self to make Copenhagen a center of scholarship. Up to that time no secular centers of learning existed in Scandinavia. Advanced education was offered in the north only under the aegis of the Catholic Church or pursued abroad, usually at the University of Paris. He declared his intention to found the first university of Scandinavia. Informed of this project Sture resolved to beat his old enemy even in this, and in 1477 the great University of Uppsala, now a seat of learning renowned throughout the world, opened its doors to its first students. Copenhagen did not have its university until a year later. Under Sture's guidance Sweden began to emerge into the modern world. Six years after the foundation of the university, Sweden was given its first printing press, also at Uppsala, and regent and archbishop gathered around this mechanical wonder, which turned out the first printed book in Swedish in 1483.

In 1481 Christian I of Denmark died, and the Danes, anxious to restore the Union, proposed that the election of a successor should be postponed until representatives of all three Scandinavian nations could meet to thrash out a new constitution for the Union. A meeting was held at Halmstad in 1483, but it was attended by delegations from Norway and Denmark only, as Sten Sture boycotted the gathering. Christian's son, John, was elected king of Norway and Denmark, but no word came from Sweden, where Sture was having trouble, as usual, with the nobility. This time, however, he held a weapon which kept

Agriculture was the chief occupation of medieval Scandinavia. Shown here are a Swedish meadow and typical Danish farm buildings.

them in check: the peasants idolized "Our Lord Sture" and whenever the nobles showed signs of serious opposition Sture called a Riksdag. The solid backing which the peasants and small merchants gave him at these meetings, of which twenty were held between 1470 and 1497, was enough to intimidate the regent's aristocratic enemies.

Peaceful progress was not destined to last long, however. In 1495 the Swedish nobles persuaded Russia to declare war on Sweden while they themselves joined forces with King John of Denmark, hoping that Sture would be unable to face a war on two fronts. The regent, however, got the better of the Russian forces in Finland; he then rounded on the Danes and the rebel Swedish noblemen, who were led by Svante Nilsson Natt och Dag. (The latter part of his name translates as Night and Day, a reflection of the blue and gold quarterings on his coat-of-arms.)

Civil war broke out in Sweden and Sture had almost subdued the rebels when John of Denmark's fleet appeared off the coast with a large sea-borne army. Once again the peasants formed up behind their "Lord." In a letter to the governors of Stockholm the peasants of Dalecarlia wrote: "Dear friends, you all know that since he became our regent we have enjoyed law and order, and peace and quiet have reigned. You also know that the provinces and castles of our Fatherland were formerly in divers hands, but that they are now united because he ventured life and property in this cause. Since he has served us so faithfully, we cannot suffer him to be driven from the regency by force."

For all the support of the local peasants, however, Sture did not command sufficient forces to risk a pitched battle against John's powerful array, and he fell back to Stockholm, where he was besieged. His pleas for reinforcements from other parts of the country seem to have gone unheeded, and in October, 1497, Sture surrendered the city in return for a full amnesty for himself and all his followers. John was at once elected king of Sweden by the triumphant noblemen who had backed him.

Their triumph did not last very long. John began to intrigue for the recognition of his son as heir, once more challenging the idea of an elective kingship. He also reneged on several other promises and achieved a *rapprochement* with Svante Nilsson's Unionists, who had been planning a well-organized rising against him. At the same time, the Danish king was disgracefully beaten in battle by a mob of rebellious peasants at Dithmarschen in Holstein and his prestige in Denmark sank to a low level. In 1501 Sten Sture was once again appointed regent, but he held office for only two years before his death in 1503.

His place as regent was taken by Svante Nilsson. Regency was now becoming a habit in Sweden and like Sture his successor had no aspirations to the throne. Theirs was the power, and with that they were content. King John, as might have been expected, refused to recognize the regent's authority, and a desultory war with Denmark limped on year after year, to the great irritation of most of the Swedish nobility, many of whose members held Danish estates through intermarriage with the Danish aristocracy. The war, which did little real damage to either side, centered around the great fortress of Kalmar, where ironically the first major attempt at Scandinavian union had been forged a century earlier. In 1509 Nilsson was forced to make peace with Denmark on terms that called for the payment of an annual tribute by Sweden.

Svante Nilsson did not even bother to pay the first installment of this levy, and in 1510 the war started up again, but this time with slightly better prospects for Sweden, since she had formed an alliance with the Hanseatic League. Nevertheless Swedish successes were few and far between and the discontented nobles were preparing to fight a civil war against Nilsson when he died in 1512. The war ended at once, and the Unionists appointed one of their number as regent. They had not, as things turned out, reckoned with Svante Nilsson's young son, Sten, who, adopting the honored name of Sture to impress the peasantry, quickly managed to seize the chief castles of Sweden. The Unionist regent was driven from office and Sten Sture the Younger succeeded in July, 1512.

A new figure now stepped upon the Scandinavian stage in the person of Prince Christian, son of King John of Denmark and Norway. Highly intelligent, brave, energetic, and statesmanlike, and, moreover, possessing an understanding and sympathy with the adversities suffered by less exalted mortals than he, his character was marred, however, by a strong streak of cruelty and cunning. Sent by his father as viceroy to Norway, the young man quickly asserted his authority. He ruthlessly stamped out attempts at rebellion and replaced Norwegian officials with Danes. But, to the general satisfaction of the people, he severely curtailed the rights of the Hanseatic merchants in Bergen and Oslo, thus effecting the beginning of the Hanse's decline in Norway.

This was an occasion for much rejoicing and at a party given in his honor by the inhabitants of Bergen, Christian met a beautiful girl who was generally known as "Dyveke," or Little Dove. The viceroy danced with Dyveke all night and, according to Arild Huitfeldt, a Danish historian of the time, "in that dance he danced away the Three Kingdoms." For Dyveke was not a simple village maiden. Behind her stood a formidable personage in the shape of her mother, Sigbrit Willemzon, a Dutch émigré of great ambition and ability and one who claimed to possess magical powers. Christian set up both ladies in Oslo and when he succeeded to the throne of Denmark and Norway in 1513 they moved with him to Copenhagen.

A year later Christian II married, by proxy, Isabella of Burgundy, the thirteen-year-old granddaughter of Emperor Maximilian, the most powerful ruler in Europe. Two years later the archbishop of Norway arrived in the Netherlands to fetch the king's child bride, but by then rumors of Christian's liaison with Dyveke had reached the emperor's ears. He insisted that the paramour and her mother be sent out of Denmark, and to this the archbishop agreed. Isabella was duly married to Christian in Copenhagen in August, 1515, but the bride soon discovered that Dyveke and her household had in fact moved only a few miles away from the capital, and she wrote angrily to her grandfather. Maximilian again insisted that Dyveke and Sigbrit leave Denmark, at which Christian sent all his wife's Dutch ladies-in-waiting back to Holland and installed Dyveke and her mother in a large house only a few yards away from his palace.

In 1517 Dyveke died suddenly, and it was believed that she had been poisoned by the governor of Copenhagen, Torben Oxe, in revenge for her rejection of him. The king arrested Oxe, only to see him acquitted by the state council. "If I had as many kinsmen on the council as he has," the king remarked bitterly, "he would never have been acquitted." Christian then assembled a summary court consisting of twelve peasants and they lost no time in condemning Oxe, declaring that "not we but Torben's own deeds find him guilty." Although the entire council, the papal legate, all the bishops, and the queen and her ladies, on their knees, pleaded that Torben Oxe be spared, he was beheaded in November, 1517.

This execution brought about a complete breach between the king and the nobility, and Christian, declaring that he could well do without the council, made Dyveke's mother, Sigbrit, his chief adviser. It was

Three Icelandic bishops, Guðmundur the Good, Saint Jón and Saint Thorlákur, are portrayed in this fifteenth-century altar frontal.

said that Sigbrit had telepathic powers "so that the king must do whatever she wished if he were within fifty miles of her," and that she was an alchemist and a witch. Whatever the truth of these accusations, it is a fact that Sigbrit was an administrative genius. She proved an admirable secretary of the treasury, saving the king great sums of money, but since she always favored the humble class from which she had herself come, and since the king valued her advice above all others, Sigbrit earned the bitter hatred of the nobility.

Christian again attacked Sweden in 1518, this time with the urging of the deposed Swedish archbishop Gustav Trolle, and the king was again beaten at the Battle of Brännkyrka. After the battle the Danish monarch suggested that Sture should meet him for a conference on his flagship, but the regent, understandably afraid of treachery, declined the invitation. Christian then declared that he was willing to meet Sture in Stockholm, provided that certain Swedish noblemen, all supporters of the regent, were prepared to accept the "hospitality" of the Danish fleet for a few days as a guarantee of Sture's good behavior during the negotiations. The list of hostages that Christian handed to Sture's heralds included a young man named Gustavus Ericsson Vasa, who came from an Uppland family that had been prominent in Swedish affairs for a century. The world was to hear much more of him in years to come. Sture agreed to Christian's terms and the hostages were rowed out to the Danish ships. No sooner were they aboard than the fleet set sail, carrying Sture's followers to Denmark as prisoners.

Having thus, as he thought, deprived the Swedish regent of most of his influential followers, Christian II assembled an army of German mercenaries, and in January, 1520, he landed in southwestern Sweden at the head of ten thousand men. Sture, as always supported by his peasants, harassed the Danish army on its march northward, and on January 19, 1520, the two armies met on the ice of the frozen Lake Asunden. Sture was seriously wounded early in battle, and when he gave up the command of the Swedish army the brave but untrained peasant-soldiers lost heart and retreated. Sture, fighting for his life, tried to reach Stockholm to ensure the defense of the city, but he died on the journey and all organized Swedish resistance to the king of Denmark was thought to be at an end.

Nevertheless, Christian's army was met all along the march by peasant-guerrillas who obstinately defended castles and fortified towns against the invader. When Christian reached Stockholm he found the citizens, led by Sture's brave widow, Christina Gyllenstierna, ready to defy him. For several months the defenders of Stockholm repulsed all Danish attacks and at last Christian concluded that only by guile could he capture the city. Among the hostages whom Christian had kidnapped earlier and taken to Denmark was the venerable bishop of Linköping, Hemming Gadh, a statesman-cleric who had played a great part in Swedish affairs and who had been outspoken in his hatred of the Danes. The old man was now brought back from Denmark and forced to negotiate on Christian's behalf with the burghers of Stockholm. Gadh advised Christina to surrender, and this she did in September, 1520, Christian promising her and all her followers full amnesty and a constitutional government in return for recognition of Christian as their king.

Christian lost no time in making the most of his hard-won victory. At the Riksdag held in Stockholm in October, 1520, he had himself proclaimed hereditary king of Sweden, in defiance of the Swedish constitution, and he was crowned at Uppsala by Archbishop Trolle. The coronation was followed by several days of festivities, and on November 7 the members of the Swedish council, a number of prominent noblemen, and the most important burgesses of Stockholm were summoned by the new king to a banquet and conference in the great hall of Stockholm Castle. The guests arrived and then, in the words of a Swedish historian of the period, "a banquet of another kind began."

Archbishop Trolle took the floor and harangued them. The Church, Trolle said, must be compensated for the indignities which she had suffered through Sture's actions, and Trolle himself should be handsomely indemnified for his deposition from the archbishopric and for the castle which Sture's men had demolished. He then named eighteen persons whom he branded as heretics responsible for these outrages; the eighteen alleged culprits were all members of the archbishop's audience, and he declared that the king's amnesty did not apply to men of this stripe.

Christina Gyllenstierna Sture who was, of course, among those present on this forbidding occasion, rose to her feet and with her customary courage declared that the action against Trolle had been taken in the

name of the whole Swedish people, and she produced the minutes of
the Riksdag to confirm this. Christian II then ordered the gates of the
castle to be closed and bolted.

When darkness had fallen two Danish noblemen followed by soldiers bearing torches and lanterns marched into the great hall and arrested all the people on the archbishop's list. Next morning a hastily summoned ecclesiastical court, under the presidency of Archbishop Trolle, declared the accused to be "manifest heretics," and at midday they were led out to a public square and beheaded. On the first day of what has come to be known as "the Stockholm Massacre," eighty-two people lost their heads, among them two bishops, fourteen noblemen, three burgomasters, fourteen members of the Stockholm city council, and twenty ordinary citizens. The executions continued the next day and were matched by those in provincial towns. Among those who fell victim to Christian's treacherous vengeance were the luckless Hemming Gadh, who was thus rewarded for having arranged the surrender of Stockholm, and the father and brother-in-law of young Gustavus Vasa, one of those kidnapped to Denmark two years previously. Christina Gyllenstierna Sture was now also sent to Denmark as a prisoner.

Christian appointed a caretaker government for Sweden, consisting of Archbishop Trolle and two of his Danish favorites, and began to march homeward. It was not difficult to follow the route of this royal progress, since it was liberally marked by gallows. As Christian later remarked complacently to the great Erasmus during a visit to Holland: "Mild measures avail nothing; the medicine that gives the body a good shaking is the best and surest." He was himself to be given a good shaking before he was much older.

CHAPTER IV

VASA AND SWEDEN'S RISE

When he kidnapped young Gustavus Vasa and carried him off to Denmark, Christian II had caught a tiger, and he did not keep him long. Vasa escaped from Danish custody in 1519 and took refuge in the city of Lübeck, where the Hanse authorities gave him refuge. In May, 1520, the young man landed on Swedish soil near Kalmar, whose fortress was again under siege by the Danes. Unperceived, Gustavus slipped through enemy lines and set about organizing resistance to the Danes in Sweden's southern provinces. In November Gustavus received news of the Stockholm Massacre, the execution of his father and other relatives, and the confiscation of the family estates. Disguised as a peasant, Gustavus made his way northward to the remote fastnesses of Dalecarlia, where he expected to find shelter while he went about his dangerous work. One of the first refuges to which he applied for hospitality proved anything but safe. Its owners betrayed Gustavus to the Danes, and for weeks he was hunted through Dalecarlia by Christian's bailiffs and men-at-arms.

Nevertheless Gustavus continued to implore the local peasants to join him in expelling the invaders. His recruiting campaign was cen-

Sixteenth-century Vadstena Castle was one of the fortified residences of the famous Swedish king Gustavus Vasa and his family.

tered in the mining district, some hundred and seventy miles northwest of Stockholm. In the little towns of Rättvik and Mora and in the villages on the shores of Lake Siljan, Gustavus delivered passionate speeches to unresponsive peasant audiences, who had not had much experience with the Danes and consequently showed no eagerness to take up arms against them. In despair Gustavus made for the Norwegian frontier.

Then the situation changed overnight, for it was rumored that Christian intended to attack Dalecarlia and to erect a gallows before every manor house in the province. At once the frightened natives remembered the fiery young man who had so recently offered to be their leader against the Danes, and swift messengers went on snowshoes to overtake him and bring him back. Gustavus returned to Mora, where the Dalecarlia notables assembled to meet him. He was proclaimed "King of the Dales and of Sweden," and young men flocked to his standard.

By April, 1521, Gustavus and his homespun army began to be taken seriously by the Danish rulers of Sweden. Didrik Slagheck, the organizer of the Stockholm Massacre, and the indomitable Archbishop Trolle led an army of Danes, stiffened by foreign mercenaries, to crush the insolent rebels. The two forces faced one another across the Dal, a long and wide estuary seventy-five miles north-northwest of Stockholm. Gustavus stood on one shore with a thousand peasants at his back, and the Danes, on the opposite shore, did not like what they saw. Depressing tales of the hardihood of these Dalecarlia rustics had reached the Danish leaders. "Men who can eat wood and drink water," Archbishop Trolle announced gloomily, "will not yield to the Devil himself," and the Danish force withdrew.

Gustavus at once launched his men in pursuit of the enemy and routed them with great loss. As always happens success brought many waverers over to Gustavus' side, including a number of noblemen with military experience who undertook to train the Swedish volunteers, now numbering fifteen thousand. At the end of April Gustavus marched on the town of Västerås, less than one hundred miles west of Stockholm, where he was met by a large force of Danish cavalry. The horsemen charged the peasant ranks again and again, but failed to break them and at last the Danes were forced to retire, leaving Gustavus in possession of their cannon, which he badly needed.

Notwithstanding these successes Gustavus' position was shaky. He had no money, only a few guns, an army almost entirely without discipline, and no navy whatever. Nevertheless the Estates of South Sweden gathered that autumn at Vadstena to elect Gustavus regent of Sweden, and Christian II began to make elaborate preparations to crush him.

By this time, however, Gustavus was much better equipped to meet the king's wrath. Lübeck, his old refuge, came to his aid with money, troops, and ships. Other Hanseatic cities, with a shrewd eye on the trade which would follow Gustavus' success and vivid memories of what Christian had done to the Hanse in Bergen many years before, contributed to the Swedish war chest. Gustavus in the course of the summer had captured a number of castles and fortified sites and was now able to besiege Stockholm. By June, 1522, when the Hanse fleet dropped anchor off the city, Gustavus had the place closely surrounded. But Stockholm was still strongly defended by Christian's occupation forces, and the battle dragged on with, apparently, little prospect of success for either side.

Civil war in Denmark finally weighted the scales in Gustavus' favor. For some time, under Sigbrit's influence, Christian II had worked to increase the power of the peasants and lower middle class at the expense of the nobility, who were jealous of their prerogatives and consequently were almost unanimous in their opposition to the king. To these enemies Christian now added the Church. The Reformation, brought to a climax by Martin Luther at the Diet of Worms in 1521, had made a great impact on Christian, who had plans for the establishment of a Danish National Church, independent of Rome, and this at once ranged every high churchman in Denmark with the nobles. Just before Christmas, 1522, three bishops and several noblemen of Jutland, in session at Vyborg, issued a declaration which claimed that Christian's tyranny and misrule had thrown his three kingdoms into misery. The signatories renounced their allegiance to Christian II and invited his uncle, Duke Frederick of Holstein, to take the Danish throne.

Christian made a rather feeble effort to negotiate with his enemies, but in April, 1523, he abandoned the attempt and with Sigbrit, his family, and a few friends sailed from Copenhagen and into an exile in Holland which was to last for eight years and reduce him to dire pov-

AGO NOBILISSIME PIE AC VENE — — ROSE DNE DOMINE MARGARET
IE NOBILITATIS AC ÆQVITISA — — RATI ERICI IOHANNIS QVE
B HONESTO TITVLO VIXIT — — RUBOHOLM ET DEPICTA
EST HÆC MEMORIA — — ANNO ETC. 1528.

At left is Gustavus I Vasa, king of Sweden and founder of the Vasa dynasty.
Above is his sister, Margareta Vasa. Both paintings hang at Gripsholm Castle.

erty. He was succeeded by the aristocracy's choice, Frederick I, who later became king of Norway as well.

As soon as the news of Christian's deposition reached Sweden the Riksdag realized that unless they quickly chose a king Frederick I would claim the Swedish throne—and they had no wish to be ruled by another German sovereign. Meeting at Strängnäs at the end of May, the Riksdag willingly chose Gustavus as their monarch, and he was proclaimed king of Sweden on June 6.

Meanwhile Christian's flight could not fail to lower the morale of his Stockholm garrison and the city surrendered to Gustavus in June on Midsummer Eve, 1523, after a siege that had lasted two years. When he entered the capital Gustavus found that hunger and disease had halved the population and that the number of tax-paying burgesses had been reduced by three quarters.

The first concern of the new ruler was to put Stockholm on its feet again. He issued peremptory orders that certain merchants from another Swedish town must settle forthwith in Stockholm, under pain of heavy punishment for refusal to do so, and that they and the survivors from the original population must at once set to work to rebuild the city. With a magnanimity which was probably little appreciated by its beneficiary, Gustavus took no worse revenge upon the pestilential Archbishop Trolle than to banish him from the realm.

The Hanse, as might have been expected of such astute businessmen, now presented their bill to Gustavus. The merchants had stipulated that, in return for their help, Gustavus would grant the Hanseatic League trading rights, and exempt them from all duties and taxes, thus giving them an effective monopoly of Swedish commerce. With great reluctance, Gustavus now honored the bargain. "Kingship," he observed ruefully after the merchants had taken leave of him, "has more gall than honey in it."

King Gustavus I was twenty-six when he ascended the Swedish throne. His accession was not welcomed abroad, where he was generally regarded as a usurper who had displaced Sweden's rightful king. However, since almost all information regarding events in Sweden reached the rest of Europe by way of Denmark, it is probable that opinion abroad owed a good deal to Danish propaganda.

This king, who united Sweden and gave her a new concept of her

place in Europe, was a well-built man of medium height, blue-eyed,
fair-haired, and with a long, wavy beard. He was, as a rule, a cheerful
extrovert, approachable and easy to talk to, and possessed of a degree
of common sense that verged on genius. Gustavus enjoyed music and
on quiet evenings liked to sing to his own accompaniment on the lute.
He was no scholar but he has left to us twenty-nine volumes of letters,
memorandums, and other documents, most of them dictated to secre-
taries, in which the workings of his mind are plainly seen. Gustavus
Vasa possessed an extraordinary memory, so that a man whom he had
met only once many years before would be astonished to be greeted
by name at a second encounter with his sovereign. Early experience had,
however, made the king deeply suspicious, and his temper, when
roused, was terrifying. He could be merciless to his enemies and that
long memory never forgot an injury. The Danes, in particular, he
never forgave.

The territory over which this remarkable young man now ruled was
not the Sweden of today. Finland continued to be an integral part of
the realm, but the territories of Skåne, Blekinge, and Halland, in the
south, were all Danish, and Bohuslän (north of today's Göteborg),
Jämtland, and Härjedalen were Norwegian (and consequently subject
to the Danish kingdom). The strait of Öresund and the Great and
Little Belt straits, which link the Baltic with the Kattegat and the
North seas, were directly or indirectly in Danish hands; and Sweden's
only guaranteed outlet to the Western world was a tiny strip of land,
ten miles wide, at the mouth of the Göta River. Here lay a small trading port, then known as Lödöse, which was to become the modern
Göteborg.

The first years of Gustavus' reign were passed in constant fear of an
invasion by Danes seeking to restore the Union of Kalmar. Nor was
Denmark the only enemy in sight; the Hanse were growing daily more
insolent in their demands. One day Gustavus meant to have a settlement with these traders which they would not enjoy, but the forces at
the king's disposal were quite inadequate, since the old national levy,
known as the *Folkuppbåd,* could not produce fighting men capable
of standing up to modern weapons and tactics. The real military
strength of the kingdom traditionally derived from feudal levies which
made the king dependent upon the cooperation of the nobility. They,

in turn, relied on the gentry to fill the ranks of royal knights, the spear-head of the Swedish army. The two classes had quarreled over the old issue of the Union, the noblemen seeking restoration and the gentle-men opposing it. With the country's defenses in this state of disarray Gustavus would have liked to hire mercenaries, but the treasury lacked the money to pay them.

There were other stresses within the kingdom. Gustavus Vasa and the Church were heading toward a showdown. During the council that had elected him king in 1523, Gustavus had attended sermons by a Swedish graduate of the University of Wittenberg, where Martin Luther held sway. Olaf Petterson, better known by the Latinized name of Olaus Petri, was a keen Lutheran and his discourses and those of his disciples had greatly impressed the royal listener, whose relations with Rome and with his high prelates at home were growing ever more strained. When he made Petri and another archdeacon of Lutheran persuasion his advisers, and then began to eye some of the Church's property, the displeasure of the clergy was strongly expressed.

Then, too, Vasa was encountering trouble from the people of Dale-carlia who, only two years earlier, had been chiefly responsible for his successful campaign for the throne. Now they threatened to depose him, complaining that he had "made light of good Swedish men and bidden Germans and Danes come into the country." Taxes were too high, the Dalecarlians said. "We see that you mean wholly to destroy us poor Swedish men, which with God's help, we will prevent—take note hereof and act accordingly."

Now he became locked in an impasse with Pope Adrian VI over who should be Sweden's archbishop. Adrian ordered that the politi-cally meddlesome Trolle be reinstated at Uppsala. Gustavus Vasa put forth his own candidate in the Swedish-born papal legate Johannes Magni. Gustavus told the pope that unless he confirmed Johannes' election as archbishop he himself would look after the affairs of the Swedish Church in future, but Pope Adrian and his successor, Clement VII, refused to budge. By now Petri was claiming that the pope was Antichrist and that the Church was robbing the Swedish people. Gus-tavus agreed. "God sent His sheep into the world to be pastured, not to be shaven and shorn," he said, and the king's leaning toward Luther-anism soon became plain for all to see.

Among those who saw it were the stubborn Dalecarlians, who in
1527 protested that the king had become "a Lutheran and a heathen."
Gustavus replied mildly that he had done no more than order that
God's word and Gospel should be preached "so that priests should no
longer deceive simple folk." This quite failed to satisfy the Dalecarlians. "At Court hereafter," their spokesman demanded, "there should
not be so many foreign and outlandish customs, with laced and bro-
caded clothes. . . . The king should burn alive or otherwise do away
with all who ate flesh on Friday or Saturday."

At this Gustavus lost his somewhat touchy temper. The Dalecarlians were told to mind their own business and not to bother their heads
about things which they did not understand. The king refused to listen
to moral lectures from peasants: "As to how I shall clothe my bodyguard and servants," he went on, "I prefer to model myself on other
monarchs, such as kings and emperors, so that they may see that we
Swedes are no more swine and goats than they are."

The Dalecarlian protest simmered down for the moment, and Gustavus was able to concentrate on the task of reforming the Church,
which, as his contemporary Henry VIII of England also discovered,
was a very profitable business for the crown, then badly in need of
infusions of cash.

But Vasa needed the support of the Estates to accomplish his ends.
He faced his problems squarely by calling a meeting of the Riksdag at
the Black Friars' Monastery in Västerås in June, 1527. He placed before them "the king's proposals," reminding them that he had taken
over the country when it was in a perilous condition. Despite the oath
of allegiance which the people had given him, he met constant ob-
struction and criticism. For this disloyalty and ingratitude, he was
prepared to abdicate, but he recommended that the next king would
have to be given a far more sizeable and permanent source of revenue
if any governmental stability was ever to be achieved. He then reiter-
ated his scheme for confiscating the lion's share of Church properties
and making their income henceforth payable to the royal treasury.

The ranking bishop Hans Brask of Linköping replied on behalf of
his fellow churchmen that only upon the pope's instructions would
they yield the lands and goods entrusted to their keeping. This caused
Gustavus to make an emotional retort in which he charged his people

with ingratitude. "I am not surprised," he said, "that the common people are maddened and disobedient; they take after such as you! When they lack rain and sunshine, they blame me for it; dearth, famine, pestilence—I am blamed for it all. For all my trouble my sole reward is that you would like to see an axe sticking in my head, though none of you dare hold its handle. . . . I tell you straight I will not be your king any longer! . . . Therefore be ready to pay me back what I have spent of my own upon the kingdom; I will then take my departure and never come back to my ungrateful fatherland!" Reportedly, the king then burst into tears and rushed out of the hall.

This virtuoso performance had the effect which the king sought. The Riksdag debated the proposal for several days. The rift between the church-nobility faction and the gentry-commoner classes growing ever more critical, Vasa refused all efforts at compromise, seeming fully prepared to step down if his terms were not met. Finally, the nobility, divided among itself and threatened by the lower classes, gave in to the king and an agreement known as the "Västerås Recess" was reached. Gustavus became supreme head of the Church, as Henry VIII did in England, and he at once took possession of all the bishops' castles and two thirds of the tithes normally paid to the Church.

By way of punishment, Brask was subsequently packed off on a bogus mission to Poland, never to return to Sweden; and two bishops who had dared to oppose the king and had tried to raise the Dalecarlian peasants against him were paraded through the streets of Stockholm seated backward on broken-down hacks, one with a crown of straw on his head, the other wearing a mitre made of rushes, while clowns leaped and tumbled beside the victims, urging the crowd to pelt and boo them.

In 1531 the exiled Christian II made his reappearance, though not for long. Under his uncle, Frederick I, the Danish nobles were allowed a free hand to oppress and plunder the common people as they chose, and the Danes began to long for Christian's return. Their longing was expressed in the "Eagle Song," which was sung everywhere and which declared that the Danes "looked to the eagle, far away in the wilderness," to protect them against the hawks that would "pluck out their feathers and down." Frederick had also seen to the severing of Denmark's ties with Rome and had supported Reformationist clergymen.

This little musician, part of a carved bench sculpture, recalls the days when troubadors entertained Swedish courtiers with their songs.

At last Christian was summoned by the Norwegian bishops to return to his country, which he vowed to restore to the Catholic faith. With Rome's backing he sailed from the Netherlands in October, 1531, but by the time he reached Norway half of his ten-thousand-man force had been lost at sea by shipwreck. The archbishop and many of the surviving nobility swore allegiance to Christian, but he was opposed by Denmark, Sweden, and the Hanseatic League, the latter sending its fleet to apprehend him. Christian, who was unsuccessfully besieging the fortress of Akershus, now experienced the kind of treachery which he had dealt others in the past. Accepting Frederick's promise of safe conduct to Copenhagen, he was in fact arrested and imprisoned. Visitors to Sönderborg Castle in south Jutland may still see the track reputedly worn in the flagstones of his solitary cell as Christian walked, hour after hour, year after year, around the table which stood in its center. The former king, however, would outlive two of his successors and die only in 1559 at the age of seventy-seven.

Frederick I of Denmark died in 1533, and the Danish Protestants, who had a strong voice among the nobility, sought to elect his elder son Christian, a keen Lutheran; the Catholics favored Frederick's younger son John. The election of the new king was postponed, leaving the Council of the Realm in charge of the government. Meanwhile the ambitious burgomaster of Lübeck, Jürgen Wullenwever, resolved to seize Denmark on behalf of the Hanse and to dismember the kingdom. He found allies among the predominately Catholic peasants, burgesses, and mayors of Copenhagen and Malmö, where resentment against the aristocracy exceeded all issues of faith. With the liberation of Christian II as the avowed aim, the peasant rebellion swept Denmark in the summer of 1534, with scores of noble estates put to the torch, and the eastern part of the country seized. In the midst of this chaos, the council proclaimed Christian III king, but the peasants of Jutland rose against him. Christian's commander, Johann von Rantzau, crushed this rising and conquered Jutland in a single month before turning to face the German invaders. In March, 1535, Christian was formally confirmed as king of Denmark and in June Rantzau smashed the Hanse army at Öxnebjerg; in that battle, Archbishop Trolle, belligerent to the last, was finally removed from contention.

Civil war continued until 1536, however, since Copenhagen still held out for Christian II and the Catholic cause. After a year's siege, Copenhagen surrendered, the triumphant nobles reduced the peasants and merchants to political impotence, and the Catholic Church in Denmark was doomed. Christian III decided to follow the example of Gustavus Vasa by seizing the wealthy estates of the Church and doing away with all aspects of ecclesiastical power in the management of government. Soon after, a Riksdag was called in Copenhagen at which Christian III established a National Protestant Church, with the king at its head. As a gesture of good will to the people, he blamed the bishops of the realm for Denmark's recent bloody feuds and ordered a general amnesty for crimes committed during the civil war by the other classes.

Christian also took advantage of the occasion to establish a hereditary monarchy in Denmark and to quench the last sparks of Norwegian independence. Henceforth, Norway was a part of Denmark. Christian's proclamation announced: "Inasmuch as the Realm of Norway is now so reduced in power that the inhabitants thereof are unable by themselves to maintain a sovereign and king, and the said Realm is nevertheless joined for all time to the Crown of Denmark . . . now therefore we have promised the Council and the nobility of Denmark that . . . it [Norway] shall hereafter be and remain subject to the Crown of Denmark, like our other provinces. . . . and hereafter shall not be called a Kingdom apart but a member of the Kingdom of Denmark, subject to the Crown of Denmark for all time." Olaf Engelbrektsson, the last Roman Catholic archbishop of Norway, tried to lead an uprising against the Danes who had swallowed his country, but the rebellion failed and the archbishop fled to Holland, taking with him the treasures and archives of Trondheim Cathedral.

Christian III proved himself a wise ruler and a good administrator. The royal revenues were tripled by the confiscation of Church property, and the king used some of this money to pay a new class of professional civil servants who set about repairing the damage caused by civil war, religious strife, and class hatred.

In Sweden Gustavus Vasa now faced the last rebellion of his reign. The king's confiscation of Church lands had not greatly troubled most Swedes, since tenants of the Church were allowed to continue their

OVERLEAF: *A peaceful country church on a Danish island in the North Atlantic*

leases undisturbed by the change of landlord. However, when Gustavus' bailiffs began imposing a prohibition against informal trade with Denmark and, furthermore, removing the Church plate from each parish in order to melt it down by the royal mint, the Swedish people were outraged, and a rebellion broke out. It began in 1542 at Småland, a region of lake and forest in south-central Sweden, under the skillful leadership of a certain Nils Dacke. Soon the rising spread to other provinces and the king's forces were regularly beaten by the rebels. Only by mustering every ounce of such strength as he could command did Gustavus suppress the revolt two years later. After this hard-won success the king called the Estates together at Västerås and they, in gratitude to the man who had earlier liberated their country, assented to a Pact of Succession which established the Vasa dynasty as the hereditary royal family of Sweden. Gustavus was to be succeeded by his eldest son Eric and his younger sons were to be given dukedoms which they would rule as vassals of the king.

The defeats suffered in what came to be known as "the Dacke War" had shown up the inefficiency of the young Swedish army, and this Gustavus now resolved to remedy. He set up detachments of infantry, each about five hundred strong, known as *fänikor* and recruited by voluntary enlistment; these units are the ancestors of Sweden's infantry regiments. The new standing army mustered fifteen thousand men, and Gustavus revived his navy by building twenty-five large men-of-war.

With the royal power now firmly established to Vasa's satisfaction, the king devoted the rest of his reign to strengthening the economy. He was tireless in supervising the affairs of his realm, traveling constantly about the country, inspecting a new barn or a shipyard with equal interest, keeping a sharp eye on the national accounts, and introducing new techniques in commerce, mining, and farming. Woe betide the tenant on one of the royal farms who neglected his holding. He was heavily punished, for his farm, the king announced again and again, "belongs to us and to Sweden."

As Gustavus' life drew to a close his son Eric gave him much cause for anxiety. The young man, notably well-educated and intelligent, was also hot-tempered, arrogant, and unstable. One conflict between them arose over Eric's decision to woo Elizabeth I of England, who had come to her throne in 1558. Gustavus told his son not to make a fool of himself, but Eric nevertheless went ahead with the organization of a costly expedition which was to go to England and lay his marriage proposal before Elizabeth. Gustavus, with his usual good sense, vetoed this excursion much to Eric's fury, but the episode increased Gustavus' doubts as to the fitness of his son to rule Sweden.

Gustavus I clearly foresaw his own impending death. In his last speech to his people on June 26, 1560, the king, now aged sixty-three, recalled the victory over Denmark nearly forty years before: "God did the work, and made me His miracle-worker through whom His almighty power should be made manifest against King Christian. . . . God gave David victory over Goliath and made him king. Thus He did with me, unworthy as I am. . . . My time is soon up. I have no need of starcraft or other prophecy thereof. I know the signs of my own body that I shall soon depart." The old king ended his address by blessing his people and commending them to God. Later that fall, Gustavus closed his eyes for the last time; he was buried in Uppsala Cathedral. The achievements of this remarkable monarch may be seen to this day. He had led Sweden from foreign bondage to independence. He had found his kingdom torn by civil strife, bankrupt and powerless in the international sense. He left it free, orderly, and prosperous. His true monument is not the ending of Danish and German domination in his youth, but the slow, patient work of reform and reconstruction which he performed, year in, year out, in peacetime. His legacy to Sweden was well summed up by Gustavus' famous grandson, Gustavus II Adolphus, who said: "This King Gustavus was the instrument by which God again raised up our fatherland to prosperity."

CHAPTER V

REFORMATION
AND RELIGIOUS WARS

Gustavus Vasa, who married three times, had four sons—Eric, who succeeded him as Eric XIV, and John, Charles, and Magnus, who became respectively dukes of Finland, Södermanland, and Östergötland. Eric, whose instability had so worried his father, was, according to France's ambassador, "very handsome and well built, marvelously accomplished, speaking French, German and Latin like his mother-tongue, excellent in drawing, singing, violin playing and mathematics." He was crowned at Uppsala in 1561 with a pomp never before seen in Sweden, and he continued to press his suit for Elizabeth I, while at the same time trying his luck with Mary Queen of Scots and a number of German princesses.

The courtship of Elizabeth, fruitless though it was, brought Sweden one lasting advantage. One of Eric's envoys, while he was biding his time in England waiting to see the queen, was served a dish of fresh-water crayfish. The Swedish emissary greatly relished these tiny lobsters and on his return to Sweden brought back several bucketfuls, alive. The English crayfish quickly settled down with the local variety in Swedish rivers and multiplied rapidly. They are now Sweden's most

Christian IV's Renaissance-style castle of Frederiksborg, which with its many associated buildings covers several islands within a lake

cherished national dish; their consumption, during the month of August only, is elevated to the status of ritual. No visitor to Sweden in that month can (or should) escape a *Kräftkalas,* or crayfish party, at which each guest devours a dozen or more crayfish, each claw, in theory, washed down by a glass of *Brännvin,* or local schnapps. For this at least, though not for much else, Sweden may be grateful to Eric XIV.

It would have been too much to hope that Denmark would allow the death of Gustavus Vasa to pass without an attempt to reassert its claim to the crown of Sweden. In 1563 after a number of complicated maneuvers, in which Duke John of Finland conspired against his half brother and was imprisoned, war broke out between Sweden and Denmark, the latter supported by Lübeck and Poland. The Swedish navy, under the celebrated admirals Jacob Bagge and Klas Horn, drove the Danish and Hanseatic fleets from the Baltic, but on land things went less well for them. The Danish army was largely composed of Germans, professional soldiers to a man. The Swedes, although they had enlisted some German and Scottish mercenaries, relied mostly on native troops, who lacked both discipline and experienced officers to impose it. The Danes were led by the redoubtable Daniel von Rantzau, who was a seasoned commander, but Eric, interested though he was in soldiering and filled though his head was with military plans, never had the courage to put his schemes to the test of battle.

Rantzau, at the head of a small but highly efficient force, marched on the town of Jönköping and, encountering no real resistance, pushed quickly northward into Östergötland, where he sacked and burned the hallowed city of Vadstena and other towns. He would, Rantzau promised, capture Stockholm and finish the war if two thousand reinforcements were sent from Denmark. Frederick II, who had recently succeeded Christian III of Denmark, never sent the fresh troops, and while Rantzau waited for them Swedish resistance stiffened. In January, 1568, the Danish general at last withdrew and managed to reach Denmark without much loss.

On the whole Sweden had the best of this conflict, thanks almost entirely to the prowess of her seamen. Frederick II, discouraged, abandoned his plan for conquest. Meanwhile, the bachelor king Eric was having a bad time in Stockholm; he described 1566 as his "unhappiest year." His able favorite Göran Persson, who was regarded by the nobility as the king's evil genius, organized an efficient secret-police system against his enemies. These spies claimed to have unearthed a plot by Eric's half brother John and Nils Sture, grandson of Sten Sture the Younger. On the basis of these rumors—for they were no more than that—Eric had Sture arrested and marched through Stockholm in mock triumph. This provoked such an outburst of rage from the nobility that Eric, who was somewhat of a coward, hastened to patch things up with Nils Sture by sending him to Lorraine on yet another of those marriage embassies. (Elizabeth I had been given up as a bad job and officially Eric's present fancy was Princess Renée of Lorraine.)

Unofficially, however, the king had quite different matrimonial plans, and he hoped that his choice of a humble bride—the daughter of an army sergeant—would give the maximum offense to the hated noblemen. She was Karin Månsdotter, a sweet and gentle girl and the only person who could soothe Eric's rages, which were growing in violence and frequency with the passage of time.

Cultivated as Eric was, he was given to sadistic games and orgies. At the celebrations which he arranged for his courtiers an unlucky guest might have an eye gouged out or an arm lopped off while the other revelers roared with laughter. At the splendid apartments at Kalmar Castle which Eric beautified for his own enjoyment, the guide will not fail to point to a carved boss in one of the great rooms on which Eric cracked his head while he was being tossed in a blanket. This mishap is said to have been the origin of his final insanity.

In the spring of 1567 Eric summoned a number of the most disaffected nobles and arrested them. Nils Sture and his father, Svante Sture, were also locked up. The king then visited Svante Sture, told him that he did not believe the truth of any of the charges against him, and begged the old man's forgiveness. This same day Eric went to the cell of Nils Sture in Uppsala Castle, and crying: "There thou art, traitor!" stabbed the prisoner several times. The king's men-at-arms then finished Sture off.

Svante Sture and many other members of leading families were murdered on the same day, and the king disappeared. Two days later he was found wandering in the woods in disguise and brought back to court. He tried to make amends to the families of the murdered men and agreed that Göran Persson should be put on trial, but he was not executed. The king himself withdrew gloomily to his aptly named castle of Svartsjö (Black Lake), but by the end of the year Rantzau's depredations in the south alarmed even the king. He reinstated Persson as his chief adviser and abandoned all attempts to conciliate the nobility.

Accordingly, Eric publicly announced his intention of marrying Karin Månsdotter, acknowledged as legitimate the children she had borne him, and declared that the Stures and the other murdered noblemen had been justly slain for the crime of *lèse-majesté,* or disrespect to the king.

This was too much for Eric's half brothers, John and Charles, who refused to attend Eric's wedding to Karin in July, 1568, or her subsequent coronation. The great noblemen of the realm met the two rebel brothers at Vadstena and renounced their allegiance to Eric XIV. The rebellion, which started in the south, soon spread to the central provinces, and the citizens of Stockholm, defying Eric's strong garrison, captured Göran Persson and handed him over to the conspirators, who tortured him elaborately and hanged him. Then the south gate of the city was flung open to the rebels, who marched triumphantly into Stockholm. Eric meekly surrendered, and in January, 1569, he was formally deposed. His eldest half brother succeeded him as John III. Eric, who by now showed clear signs of madness, was imprisoned. He died on a Thursday in February, 1577, at Örbyhus prison, after eating a bowl of pea soup probably poisoned on John's orders. Swedes still mark the occasion by making *ärter med fläsk* (pea soup with pork), a traditional Thursday dish.

Denmark at this time was receiving, though in no very hospitable fashion, a famous and tragic exile, James Hepburn, the fourth earl of Bothwell. A man of dark passions and unlimited ambition, he had been brought to trial on charges of murdering Lord Darnley, the feeble consort of Mary Queen of Scots. Bothwell and Mary did in fact marry but, although he was acquitted in 1567, Scotland was no longer a safe place for him to live and he fled first to the Shetland Islands and then to the Continent.

Two centers of Danish commerce in the Caribbean—Frederiksted (top) and Christiansted (bottom) on Saint Croix—are shown here in later drawings.

In his youth the earl had married a Norwegian noblewoman, and this early match was now to have fatal consequences for him. The ship in which he was traveling, disguised as a sailor, was wrecked off the Norwegian coast and the identity of the celebrated survivor was soon discovered. Bothwell's Norwegian wife at once accused the earl of bigamy, because of his marriage to Mary of Scotland, and he was arrested. Frederick II of Denmark was delighted at the capture of a man who, rightly used, might have all kinds of diplomatic possibilities, and Bothwell was imprisoned first at Malmö and then at Dragsholm, on the west coast of the island of Zealand, some fifty miles from Copenhagen. There he was immured under conditions which grew steadily more severe. Half-starved and utterly isolated, the once dashing earl died insane, at the age of forty-two, in April, 1578.

The remains of this unhappy man may still be seen in the church of Faarevejle, two miles from Dragsholm. Bothwell was given decent burial in the churchyard of the little village, but at some time in the 1880s the casket was exhumed. The earl's skull and locks of his hair were taken as souvenirs by the citizens of Dragsholm. In 1949 belated amends was made to the earl. His remains were reassembled and now lie in a glass-fronted casket in a bare chamber beneath Faarevejle Church. The earl, dressed in white robes, his head resting on a green satin pillow, still seems to defy his enemies, his limbs unrelaxed, his jaws set in a snarl.

Denmark and Sweden were now at peace. By a treaty signed in Stettin in 1570 Frederick II and John III renounced their respective claims upon the territories of one another, but Denmark retained her mastery of the entrance to the Baltic, and all foreign ships passing through Öresund were obliged to strike their topsails to Danish men-of-war in acknowledgment of this fact.

Frederick II now devoted himself to the arts of peace. Denmark was in the full bloom of the Reformation, and intellectual activity there made it the most progressive country in the north—far ahead of Sweden, for example, where the break with Catholic civilization had brought isolation from the Continent and reactionary thinking in its wake. By contrast, Copenhagen's university was flourishing—absorbing all the new ideas emerging in the south and contributing some of its own, especially in the sciences.

Foremost among Denmark's scholars was a young nobleman, Tycho Brahe, whose brilliant career was launched when he discovered a new star in the heavens and proceeded to make careful observations which he published in 1573 in a landmark pamphlet entitled *De nova stella.* Frederick became Tycho Brahe's patron, giving him the island of Hven, in Öresund, and a princely income. There the astronomer built observatories, workshops, printing facilities, and a center for students who came from all over Europe to learn of his discoveries. Undoubtedly, the most important legacy to come out of twenty years of research undertaken there was the new approach to scientific knowledge—in which it was established for all time that the basis of all science is precise observation and the systematic compilation of data, a principle which had been largely ignored until then. Brahe was not, however, a withdrawn scholar. He was a great drinker and brawler, a keen fisherman and hunter. He had lost the tip of his nose in a youthful duel, and had replaced it with a piece of solid silver. A man of great arrogance, he eventually quarreled with King Frederick's successor, Christian IV, and spent his last years exiled in Prague. Denmark's loss was the larger world's gain. One of Brahe's assistants at Prague, Johannes Kepler, was later to reveal the basic laws of planetary motion.

Frederick II also left behind him a solid memorial which, thanks to the publicity given to it by William Shakespeare, is visited by almost every traveler to Denmark. Between 1580 and 1592 the great castle of Kronborg was built at Helsingör, a few miles north of Copenhagen, its purpose to keep a sharp eye on ships entering the narrows which (today) separate Denmark and Sweden and to enforce the payment of tolls. This is the Elsinore Castle of Shakespeare's *Hamlet,* and it had been standing just a few years when the play was written. The only clue to the identity of the real Hamlet is given by a thirteenth-century chronicler, Saxo Grammaticus, who writes of a legendary Danish prince named Amleth about whom nothing much is known. Visitors to Kronborg who are shown "Hamlet's Grave" are entitled to look with a great deal of suspicion, for no actual Hamlet ever lived there.

Did Shakespeare ever visit the new castle? Most experts agree that he did not, yet it is known that the acting company sponsored by the earl of Leicester toured Denmark from England in 1586–87 and that they acted at Kronborg. Since this event took place during what is

EFFIGIES TYCHONIS BRAHE O. F.
ÆDIFICII ET INSTRUMENTORVM
ASTRONOMICORVM STRVCTORIS
A° DOMINI 1587 ÆTATIS SVÆ 40

known as the "mystery period" of Shakespeare's life, of which we know little, it is surely possible that the great poet, who was also an actor, was a member of this company. In any case the earl of Leicester's players must certainly have had plenty to say about the fine new castle on their return to London and Will Shakespeare may have decided upon the location of his tragedy from their glowing accounts of what is still one of Europe's great palaces.

Meanwhile Sweden's era of peace with Denmark gave the Swedes an opportunity to fight an indecisive and intermittent war against Ivan the Terrible of Russia from 1570 until 1583. King John III was no soldier, but he was well served by his French-born general Pontus de la Gardie, who saw in this not very lethal war a chance to give the Swedish army the training which it so badly needed. The war was fought for the possession of Estonia and Latvia and control of the eastern Baltic trade routes. In 1578 King John allied himself with Poland's King Stephen Báthory, who had his own reasons for containing the Muscovite state. Báthory invaded Russia and the war at last ended with Russia once again bottled up and Sweden master of the Baltic and Estonia. At the end of 1586 Stephen Báthory died and John III was encouraged to nominate his own son Sigismund to succeed him. The following August, a hard-fought election campaign concluded with the twenty-one-year-old Sigismund III Vasa on the Polish throne. John III died in 1592 with some solid achievements behind him. During his reign the Finns were granted something approaching self rule and Finland became a Swedish grand duchy. Also to his credit, the king had a passion for architecture and was a keen antiquarian. John built castles at Stockholm, Uppsala, and Vadstena and he restored and rebuilt the country's cathedrals.

The reign of John III was further marked by a quarrel with the pope, who was determined that Sweden should return to the Catholic faith. King John tried to temporize by introducing a new liturgy, known as "The Red Book," with a strong bias toward Catholicism, but he insisted that the Swedish clergy should be allowed to marry and that the worship of saints should be forbidden. On these rocks negotiations with Rome foundered. With King John dead, however, and his son Sigismund III of Poland, a fervent Roman Catholic, due to succeed him on the Swedish throne, the religious question took on new signifi-

In this wood engraving, the famous astronomer Tycho Brahe directs an assistant in his observatory on the Danish island of Hven.

cance. John's younger brother, Duke Charles, called the royal council, the nobles, and leading clergymen to a meeting at Uppsala in March, 1593. The conferees at the three-week-long meeting were agreed in recognizing the Bible as the only guiding authority of the true faith. John III's "Red Book" was replaced by the old Lutheran liturgy and the assembly denounced the "grievous errors" of the pope. No faith but Lutheranism would henceforth be worshiped publicly. In the words of its chairman: "Now is Sweden become one man and we have all one Lord and one God."

Sigismund, in Poland, was furious when news of the Uppsala meeting reached him. He sailed for Sweden, bringing with him a large retinue of Roman Catholics, headed by an unscrupulous and clever papal nuncio. Soon Mass was being celebrated in Stockholm, in contravention to the Uppsala declaration. In January, 1594, when the Riksdag met in Stockholm for the purpose of crowning Sigismund, he was warned by his uncle Charles that unless he agreed with the decisions of the Uppsala meeting the members of the Riksdag would be sent home and there would be no coronation. On February 19 Sigismund yielded and was crowned on the same day, but he wrote a secret protest which was sent to Rome. In July Sigismund returned to Poland and Duke Charles, Gustavus Vasa's third son, resumed the effective rule of Sweden, although his nephew refused to appoint him regent.

Queen Maria Eleonora and her husband King Gustavus II Adolfus of Sweden

To regularize his position Charles summoned the Riksdag to Söderköping in October, 1595, and received its authority to rule as regent. At once all Catholic priests and nuns were expelled from Sweden. The change of religion naturally led to some confusion in simple minds, as exemplified, for instance, by what happened at Kalmar in 1596. (If some people regard Sweden as a "permissive" country today, they might consider what happened there nearly four hundred years ago.) The people of Kalmar and the province surrounding it suddenly decided that marriage was out of date and they would do without it. The scandalized bishops had sinning couples dragged to the altar and married willy-nilly. Often as extra punishment, these wayward sheep were flogged, ducked in the sea or the nearest lake, pinioned together in church in a position of sexual intercourse, and otherwise invited by persuasive means to see the error of their ways. It was not long before the archbishop began to be overwhelmed by complaints that the married lives of many of the partners united under these somewhat rigorous conditions were not working out very well: husbands thrashed their wives, wives scratched out their husbands' eyes. The archbishop sought the advice of the regent, whose habit of siding with the lesser gentry and peasants in disputes with the upper classes had earned him the epithet "Peasant King." "Serves you right," replied Charles, cynically. "Why did you ever make them marry?"

In 1597 most influential members of the Swedish nobility, heartily disliking Charles' rule, had moved to Poland and were urging King Sigismund to return to Sweden and punish his uncle. Sigismund tried to enlist Danish and Spanish support for this adventure, but without success. Nevertheless he landed at Kalmar in July, 1598, and set about the subjugation of Charles. Although Spain had refused its active assistance, that country and the whole of Catholic Europe had great hopes that this expedition would assuage memories of the English defeat of the Spanish Armada in 1588 and give fresh impetus to the Catholic cause.

Sigismund's army advanced northward and occupied Linköping, while Charles marched into Östergötland to meet him. The two armies clashed at Stångebro on September 25, 1598, in a fierce battle which Charles won. Sigismund agreed to an armistice under whose terms the Polish troops were to leave Sweden, he was to come to Stockholm and rule the country according to Swedish law, and the Riksdag would judge the quarrel between him and his uncle. No sooner was this agreement signed than Sigismund broke it by refusing to come to Stockholm. Instead he sailed for Poland, leaving a strong garrison at Kalmar, which Charles at once besieged and forced to surrender.

By now the regent, rather naturally, had suffered more than enough of his nephew, and in the summer of 1599 the Riksdag met in Stockholm to formally depose Sigismund, who was declared to be a papist, an oath-breaker, and an enemy of Sweden. Charles, who already styled himself "Hereditary Prince of Sweden," conceded that Sigismund's son, Valdemar, might succeed his deposed father on condition that he be sent to Sweden and given a Protestant education. But Sigismund made no reply to this demand. The Riksdag, assembled at Linköping in March, 1600, accordingly proclaimed the regent to be king as Charles IX, and declared that Sigismund and his heirs had forfeited all rights to the crown. At the same time several members of the Swedish Council who had taken refuge in Poland and had been surrendered to Charles under the armistice terms, were put on trial at Linköping and prosecuted by Charles in person. Some of the accused were pardoned, but four who refused to recant were publicly beheaded in what has come to be known as "the Bloodshed of Linköping." It may be argued that Charles was forced to take these stern measures in defense of the Lutheran Church and of his father's lifework. Sweden stood in constant danger of foreign intervention in both its political and religious affairs. In preserving the unity of the country he paved the way for Sweden's emergence in the seventeenth century as a great European power.

Charles IX celebrated his accession to the throne by invading Latvia and thus set a match to the smouldering resentment of Sigismund and his Polish subjects. War broke out and the Swedes suffered a series of painful defeats, but Charles and Jacob de la Gardie (son of the military hero who had served John III) managed to prevent a Polish invasion of Sweden. The war would drag on for seventeen years, including a brief period of alliance between Sweden and Russia.

Meanwhile, the throne of Denmark had passed from Frederick II, who died in 1588, to his ten-year-old son Christian IV. The boy came of age in 1596 and showed promise of becoming a remarkable ruler.

A young man of extraordinary energy, he was both a good military commander and zealous in the cause of Denmark's economic growth. He was fortunate in directing the state at a time when its agricultural produce was demanding high prices in international markets and the nation's treasury was in a strong and stable condition. State planning in industry, tariff controls, postal services, the creation of new towns, and even a tentative entry into the West's race for overseas colonies were started. Under Christian IV, Denmark also enjoyed one of its most creative building booms. The king took an active interest in architecture, soliciting the advice of both foreign and native architects, but contributing enough of his own personal taste to create a peculiarly Danish Renaissance style, which is revealed in the castles of Koldinghus, Frederiksborg, and Rosenborg, the Copenhagen Arsenal, and Kristianstad's Trinity Church among the most notable achievements of his reign. To him Copenhagen owes much of its present beauty, and Christiania (now Oslo) its existence, since Christian founded the city and gave it his name. He was, however, more than a little eccentric,

A Russian map delineating the water routes from Moscow to western Europe in the sixteenth and seventeenth centuries

much given to pleasure, a great womanizer. His memory is cherished today in Denmark and, on the whole, with good reason.

However, Christian IV never lost sight of his political objectives. He made up his mind to take advantage of Charles' difficulties at home and abroad, and in April, 1611, Denmark launched an attack on Sweden. There were many grounds on which Christian could pick a quarrel with his neighbor, but he chose as his chief complaint Sweden's establishment of the port of Göteborg, on the site of the old fishing village of Lödöse, and Charles' grant to the Dutch of special privileges there.

Charles expected the Danes to launch their main attack against Göteborg, but instead Christian concentrated his forces against Kalmar. The city was soon captured, but the great fortress held out until it was surrendered by treachery in October, 1611. This was more than Charles could bear, and in a furious rage he challenged Christian to single combat. "Herein," the challenge ran, "if you fail we shall no longer consider you an honorable man or soldier." Christian treated this message with contempt, for Charles IX was now a sick man; he had already suffered two heart attacks. The Dane called Charles a "paralytic dotard" and advised him to "stay at home by the fire with your nurse." This reverse, followed by insult, may have hastened his death. King Charles died on November 30, 1611, leaving his kingdom in the worthy hands of his seventeen-year-old son Gustavus Adolphus, who had for some time been acting as his father's deputy.

The young man who came to the Swedish throne as Gustavus II Adolphus was, by any standards, a gifted ruler. He won hearts by his good manners and pleasant personality, and to these assets he added those conferred by a first-class education. Besides Swedish, Gustavus spoke German, Latin, Italian, Dutch, Russian, Polish, and Spanish. At the age of thirteen he was already discussing affairs of state with his father's advisers and with foreign ambassadors; two years later he opened the Riksdag with a speech from the throne and was administering the affairs of his own duchy. The young duke was introduced to the hardships and techniques of war at an early age, and he made a study of warfare with results which were to startle all Europe. His appearance was striking; he was tall, with great breadth of shoulder and very fair hair, which caused the Italians to christen him *Il Re d'Oro*—"the Golden King." Few monarchs have combined personal charm, intelligence, and good looks as did Gustavus Adolphus.

The young king quickly showed his mettle. The Danes had followed their success at Kalmar by an attack on Göteborg, which they burned to the ground, and they planned then to converge on the important town of Jönköping by a pincer movement executed by two columns of troops. Thence Christian intended to push on northeastward to Stockholm, where his army would have the support of the Danish fleet. Gustavus Adolphus soon put a stop to this project. Under his leadership Swedish resistance took on fresh vigor and the Danes, already somewhat exhausted by their strenuous campaign, were driven back. Christian's brother-in-law, King James I of England, offered both sides his mediation (heavily weighted, for family reasons, in favor of Denmark), and in 1613 peace was concluded at the Swedish town of Knäred. Its terms included the cession of Lapland to Denmark and the payment by Sweden of a very heavy indemnity; to pay the bill Gustavus was forced to confiscate most of Sweden's silverware, even his own.

The war against Russia still went on, however, and although the Swedish forces under Jacob de la Gardie repeatedly defeated much larger Russian armies, the tsar was always able to find fresh troops, as the Swedes were not.

War was ended, once again, through the mediation of James I. But the conditions of the 1617 peace, signed in the Russian village of Stolbova, were more favorable to Sweden than those which she had accepted at Knäred. Russia made large cessions of Finnish territory, renounced her claims on Estonia and Latvia, and paid Sweden an indemnity. Soon after the conclusion of peace Gustavus Adolphus was formally crowned in Stockholm. He at least had learned the lesson of the Russian war and realized that Sweden, with about one thirtieth of Russia's population, could never hope to withstand a full-scale Russian assault. In his coronation speech, however, Gustavus pointed out that, thanks to the terms of Stolbova, Sweden was now protected to the east by a barrier of marshes, rivers, and lakes, notably Lake Ladoga. "I hope to God," the king said, "the Russians will not find it easy to skip over *that* brook!"

Sweden enjoyed four years of peace after Stolbova, and Gustavus used them well. His position was one which his predecessors would in some ways have envied, for he was far better served than they had been. Swedish noblemen had by now taken to foreign travel and returned to their own country with a knowledge of the world and its ways which Gustavus Vasa's nobility had totally lacked. Gustavus Adolphus consequently found himself surrounded by clever, sophisticated young men, eager to help him in the government of the country, and he hastened to pardon many who had been exiled by his father and to bring them back to their own country. In Count Axel Oxenstierna, Gustavus' senior by eleven years, the king found an admirable chancellor who advised him wisely throughout his reign. Gustavus was an impulsive man with a hot temper, and Oxenstierna, cool, mature, and reflective as he was, made an ideal counterweight to his king. On one occasion Gustavus said to his chancellor: "If my ardour were not there to thaw you out you would have frozen into an iceberg long ago." This joke provoked Oxenstierna to answer in kind: "If my coldness had not moderated your heat," he replied, "Your Majesty would long ago have been consumed by fire!"

One of Gustavus' first acts after his coronation was to establish full parliamentary government in Sweden. The Riksdag was to be composed of representatives of the four estates of the realm. The First Estate, the nobility, had as its spokesman the Marshal of the Diet, or *Landtmarskalk,* while the three lower estates—clergy, burgesses, and peasants—were led by the archbishop of Uppsala. The king granted privileges to the nobility only in return for definite obligations to serve the state, and the lesser gentry were promoted to the First Estate if they showed ability. In 1619 Göteborg was rebuilt and the king called in a Dutch industrialist, Louis De Geer, to start large-scale mining and working of Sweden's great deposits of iron ore. De Geer, originally from Liège but settled in Amsterdam, brought to Sweden many Calvinist Walloons (as the French-speaking Belgians are still called), who settled down happily with their Lutheran neighbors and were soon absorbed into the population. These skilled immigrants developed the mines and ironworks at Finspång and Leufsta and a large brass foundry at Norrköping. Gustavus' attempts to establish regular trade with America and the Far East were less successful.

One of the king's most notable acts in this time of peace was to set up a supreme court in Stockholm, from whose judgments appeal might still be made to the king. Gustavus laid down strict standards for the

objectivity of this tribunal. "If any judge acts with a view to please the
King or any one else," he warned the jurists, "the King will have him
flayed, his skin nailed up in court, and his ears on the stocks!"

The years of peace ended in 1621. Sigismund of Poland, far from
reconciled to his loss of the Swedish crown, had refused to recognize
Gustavus as king of Sweden and referred to him contemptuously as
"the duke of Södermanland," a title which he insisted on using in
negotiations with his cousin. Gustavus was not the man to put up with
this behavior and his army laid siege to Riga. Gustavus' own efforts
matched those of his soldiers. Like all good officers he never asked his
troops to do anything that he was not ready to do himself, and the king
wielded spade and pick as briskly as any of his men in digging entrenchments around the beleaguered city. A Scottish officer who was
privileged to serve him later wrote, "Such a Generall would I gladly
serve; but such a Generall I shall hardly see; whose custome was: to
bee the first and last in danger himselfe, gayning his officers' love, in
being the companion both of their labours and dangers." Riga fell
after a short struggle and the Swedes occupied the whole of Latvia.

Gustavus' entry into what is now known as the Thirty Years' War
was not dictated simply by spite against Poland. The term "Thirty
Years' War" is in itself misleading. The conflict in fact lasted for
fifty years—from 1610 until 1660—and it was, basically, a struggle
between the Catholic Austrian house of Hapsburg, led by the Holy
Roman Emperor, and the Protestant princes and cities of Germany,
who opposed Catholic rule. In 1619 the Holy Roman Emperor Ferdinand II and Duke Maximilian of Bavaria, the leaders of the Catholic
forces in Europe, had driven Elector Frederick V, of the Palatinate,
from the throne of Bohemia and were now inflicting savage punishment upon all German Protestants. The elector was the son-in-law of
James I of England, and James appealed to Denmark and Sweden to
reward his recent efforts as a mediator by supporting Frederick.

Gustavus was at this time engaged (as was Christian of Denmark)
in trying to secure complete control of the Baltic, and he did not for a
moment intend to be diverted from his purpose by a war in Germany.
Accordingly he treated the advances of the British ambassador in Stockholm with great politeness but did not commit himself. Christian, on
the other hand, coveted German territory as a desirable addition to his

kingdom and eagerly accepted James' offer to finance a Danish campaign in Germany. At the head of an army composed largely of German mercenaries Christian marched into Germany in 1625 and in August, 1626, he was decisively beaten at Lutter am Barenberge, near Brunswick. Christian's German allies promptly abandoned him to his fate and soon the emperor's great commander, Albrecht von Wallenstein, swept into Jutland, plundering the "heretics" at will and behaving with a cruelty that Danes have never forgotten. Christian, who was quarreling with his council on the island of Fyn, was powerless to succor his subjects.

The Catholic plan was that Jutland should be handed over to Spain, while Poland was to be helped in her conflict with Sweden and the Protestant Dutch were to be excluded from their favored trading rights at Göteborg. Wallenstein, creeping ever closer to Sweden, besieged Stralsund, on the German mainland, swearing to capture the port "though it were slung with chains between earth and heaven," and this was the signal for Swedish intervention. A force of Gustavus' crack Scottish mercenaries under the command of Sir Alexander Leslie beat Wallenstein signally and forced him to retreat. Gustavus Adolphus thus challenged the Holy Roman Empire.

Poor Christian, in the meanwhile, was summoned to a peace conference at Lübeck from which a Swedish delegation was ignominiously excluded. The Holy Roman Emperor demanded that Denmark submit to terms so harsh that Wallenstein felt bound to modify them. The provinces which Wallenstein had conquered were restored to Denmark on condition that she abandon the Protestant cause, whereupon Gustavus Adolphus sought out Christian and tried to put some backbone into him. But the king of Denmark was now as gloomy as he had once been optimistic and urged Gustavus not to interfere.

"Your Highness may be sure of this," Gustavus Adolphus boasted, "that be it who it will, who acts thus against us, Emperor or King, Prince or Republic, or a thousand devils, we shall seize one another by the ears so hard that the hairs shall stand on end!" But Christian, utterly disheartened, refused to defy the emperor again.

The persecution of the Protestants in Germany had now reached such alarming proportions that Gustavus Adolphus could no longer watch unmoved. He determined to go to their aid, but first he was care-

This rather whimsical view of a sauna was included in the seventeenth-century Russian work Medicine for the Soul.

ful to make peace with Poland. A truce with Poland which was to last for six years was accordingly arranged through French and English mediation, and Gustavus Adolphus was free to give all his attention to a settlement with the emperor Ferdinand and his Catholic allies.

By now, thanks to Christian's disastrous campaign in Germany, Gustavus ruled over a Sweden which was supreme in the Baltic, but he was anxious to add German territories on the southern coast of that sea to his dominions, and these he might hope to obtain by a successful war in Germany. Strong as motives of religion were in the king's mind, his resolution to go to war rested also upon these more practical considerations. He feared, moreover, that the imperialists, having vanquished the German Protestants, would then turn upon the Protestant Swedes and he urged upon the Riksdag the advantages of what would now be called a "preventive war." The Riksdag agreed. "It is better," one of their leaders said, "that we tether our horses to the enemy's fence than he his horses to ours."

The army with which the king of Sweden proposed to invade Germany was quite unlike any Europe had seen before. Each Swedish province was required to provide one or two regiments, according to its population, and gaps were filled by local drafts. Although the king was anxious that his forces should as far as possible be Swedish, his own country was not able to furnish all the men he needed. The total population of Sweden at this time was about 850,000, with another 350,000 vassals in Finland, and it was clear that even the "total mobilization" (by the standards of the time) which Gustavus had organized could not produce a purely Swedish army capable of waging a major war in Europe. The Swedish regiments were therefore supplemented by well-trained bodies of Scottish and German mercenaries. (After the war, the Scots, in particular, would settle in Sweden and prosper greatly, so that many of Sweden's first families now bear Scottish names—Leslie, Douglas, Hamilton, Munro, and so on.)

From his study of war Gustavus had concluded that mobility was the prime requirement of a modern army. All equipment, therefore, was as light as possible, the flintlock muskets easily handled and quickly loaded, the artillery astonishingly easy to maneuver. Hitherto mounted guns had been established in fixed positions from which they could not be moved, but Gustavus' "flying artillery" could easily be switched

from one position to another, to the bewilderment and confusion of
his opponents. Gustavus Adolphus, in fact, introduced the modern concept of tactics, and the old methods of warfare, derived from the Middle Ages, were swept away by the blast of Swedish cannon and muskets.

By the summer of 1630 Gustavus was ready to take to the field. There were, he told his council, only two courses open to him after the miserable defection of Christian IV—to remain passive and hope that the storm would blow over or to meet the storm with every man he could muster at his back. The council agreed that the latter answer was the right one. Oxenstierna, in later years, called the decision "the inspiration of genius."

Gustavus summoned the Estates to meet in Stockholm and told them of his intentions. Then, holding in his arms his only child, Christina, aged three, the king solemnly took leave of his people. "Since it generally happens," Gustavus said in his farewell speech, "that the pitcher goes so often to the well that at last it breaks, thus also it will fall out with me that I, who in many dangers have needs shed my blood for the welfare of Sweden, though hitherto God has spared my life, yet at last I must lose it. Therefore I do commend you all to God's protection, wishing that after this wretched and troublesome life we may meet each other in the heavenly life which the Lord has prepared for us with joy everlasting."

Next day the king embarked for Germany.

CHAPTER VI

AGE OF
ABSOLUTISM

Gustavus Adolphus landed on the island of Rügen on June 24, 1630, and at once began to establish bases in Pomerania through which his lines of communication with Sweden could be maintained. The king was very much a David challenging the Catholic Goliath, for he embarked upon his campaign virtually without allies. Cardinal Richelieu of France, whose primary aim was to humble the Hapsburgs, had indeed offered Gustavus an alliance and a French subsidy, but the purposes behind the offer were so clearly in the interests of France rather than the Protestant cause that Gustavus refused. The refusal did not last long, for Richelieu continued to proffer money and Gustavus continued to need it. By the Treaty of Bärwalde, signed in January, 1631, France undertook to pay Sweden a million *livres* a year, and in return Gustavus promised to "fight for the liberty of the German princes oppressed by the emperor."

By the spring of 1631 the Swedish army had cleared Mecklenburg of imperial troops and Gustavus began his march southward along the Oder River. Fortunately for him Wallenstein, the emperor's chief officer, had quarreled with his master and was now sulking on his

The spires of Sweden's Uppsala Cathedral, begun in 1260 and still the largest church in Scandinavia, are reflected in the Fyris River.

estates in Bohemia, but even without Wallenstein's opposition the task which lay before Gustavus was daunting enough, for the count of Tilly, who subsequently commanded the imperial forces, was also a highly skilled general.

Tilly's army was besieging Magdeburg and Gustavus tried to persuade the elector of Brandenburg to join him, but that potentate hesitated to take the plunge. His indecision was paid for by the fall of Magdeburg to Tilly's forces, who burned and looted the city. Gustavus, feeling that this lesson would not be lost on other German princes, turned toward Saxony, whose elector had also been unable to make up his mind. Now the Saxons begged for Gustavus' help. His army, bolstered by the forces of German Protestant rulers, numbered forty thousand, with no more than half of them Swedes.

On September 7, 1631, the opposing armies faced one another near the village of Breitenfeld, north of Leipzig. Although the Saxons were routed in the first shock of battle, Gustavus' modern weapons and the excellent discipline of his troops soon proved their value. The imperialists were utterly defeated, and the Protestant victory at Breitenfeld sent a shudder through Catholic Europe. It was, said good Catholics, "as though God Himself had turned Lutheran," and they awaited anxiously the next move of the Swedish champion. Oxenstierna advised Gustavus to dictate peace terms after this great success. The king, he said, should march to Vienna and there, at the very heart of the empire, bring the emperor to heel. Gustavus, however, feared to leave Tilly at his rear. He sent the elector of Saxony into Bohemia while he led his forces toward the Rhine. The advance of Gustavus' army was a triumphal progress. Almost every city along the line of march opened its gates to the Swedes and those that did not were sacked and looted. Marienburg-am-Main suffered this fate and Swedish soldiers, it was said, collected gold coins by the hatful.

Having cleared the Palatinate of its imperialist garrisons, mostly Spanish, Gustavus settled down for the winter at Frankfurt-am-Main. He was now in command of an army of one hundred thousand men, of whom only a fifth were Swedes. The elector of Saxony had occupied Prague and the Protestant front extended from the Rhine to the Moldau. Every Protestant prince in Germany hurried to Gustavus' court, as did ambassadors from all over Europe. People began to talk of "the

Protestant Emperor" and grandiose plans were hatched at Frankfurt, the most ambitious of which proposed that Gustavus should cross the Alps and seize the very keys of Saint Peter from the pope.

Gustavus, however, remained a practical soldier. He divided his forces into four armies, and in the spring of 1632 one of them suffered a minor reverse at Tilly's hands. At once Gustavus was on the move with his main army, which drove Tilly back into Bavaria with Gustavus in pursuit. Crossing the Danube, Gustavus found Tilly awaiting him on the other side of the river. With his "flying artillery" in action, Gustavus' army was relatively mobile and it pounded the heart out of the enemy. Tilly's leg was shattered by a cannon ball early in the battle, and his troops, losing courage, took to their heels. Two weeks later Tilly died and Wallenstein, his differences with the emperor now composed, once more took command of the emperor's army. He soon cleared the Saxons out of Bohemia and marched on Nuremberg, seeking to lure Gustavus northward out of Bavaria.

Wallenstein's plan succeeded. Gustavus marched to relieve Nuremberg and for two months the Swedish and imperial armies, both heavily entrenched, glared at one another outside the city. At last Gustavus launched an attack on Wallenstein's lines and was heavily repulsed. The Swedes and their allies turned southward toward Austria, hoping that Wallenstein would follow them. The imperial general raised his siege of Nuremberg, but only because his troops were short of supplies; and instead of chasing Gustavus southward, he marched toward the north, threatening his enemy's lines of communication with Sweden. By a series of forced marches, Gustavus pushed quickly through Thuringia and at last came up with the enemy as Wallenstein was settling into winter quarters at Lützen, in Saxony.

On November 6, 1632, Gustavus hurled his army against Wallenstein, only to see the Swedish infantry overwhelmed. The king restored the situation by cavalry charges and then, hearing that his right flank was in danger of being crushed, led the cavalry, through thick mist, to the relief of his hard-pressed soldiers. Suddenly a large force of Austrian cavalry surged out of the fog and surrounded Gustavus' party. The king's horse was wounded, Gustavus' own arm broken by a musket ball, and, as he tried to ride out of the turmoil, he was shot in the back. The sabers of Croatian cavalry at last gave Gustavus II Adolphus the death in battle which he had always expected and for which, perhaps, he had hoped. His battered, bloody body was later recovered, stark naked, from beneath a pile of corpses. He was thirty-eight. The death of their king, far from disheartening the Swedish army, seemed to give it a vengeful determination which was too much for the enemy. As night began to fall, Wallenstein retreated, leaving twelve thousand dead and wounded on both sides on the field.

Catholic Europe celebrated the death of the Protestant champion as a signal of divine favor. *Te Deums* were solemnly sung in Madrid and Vienna, and the Spanish court was entertained by a miracle play entitled "The Death of the King of Sweden." The Protestants were correspondingly downcast, but Gustavus had nevertheless altered the course of history and their cause was safe, thanks to him. Napoleon, not a bad judge of such matters, later declared that Gustavus had revolutionized the art of war and even his enemies could not withhold their admiration. Gualdo Priorato, an Italian who had fought against Gustavus, wrote: "No prince was ever so beloved as he was. . . . no general was obeyed with greater affection and readiness. He made no difference by treating Protestants more leniently than Catholics. . . . He declared that they were all beings created by God, and that he regarded each one who diligently observed the rules of authority as possessing a good faith." This great king lies today in the Riddarholms Church in Stockholm. His tomb bears the inscription *Moriens triumphavit*—"In his death he was triumphant."

Gustavus left Sweden a great power, but the succession presented difficulties. Christina, his heiress, was only six years old and her mother, Maria Eleonora of Brandenburg, although a very beautiful woman, was eccentric and unbalanced. Oxenstierna therefore ruled Sweden as head of a Council of Regency, although much of his time was spent in Germany, where the Protestant princes needed constant encouragement and support. The command of the army went to Oxenstierna's son-in-law, Gustavus Horn, who lost his most dangerous opponent on the battlefield when Wallenstein was murdered in February, 1634.

That same year, nevertheless, saw the virtual annihilation of the bulk of the Swedish army at Nördlingen, in Bavaria. Horn was taken prisoner in this battle and at once the German Protestant coalition began to fall apart. By skilled diplomacy Oxenstierna managed to

This painting records a pyrotechnic display at Narva in 1649; it celebrated Sweden's gains at the Peace of Westphalia ending the Thirty Years' War.

maintain some semblance of unity, and in October, 1636, the new commander-in-chief, Johan Banér, restored the reputation of Swedish arms by a smashing victory at Wittstock, followed by a brilliant defensive campaign against forces which outnumbered his own by more than four to one and a successful retreat into Pomerania, where Banér was able to reinforce and re-equip his troops. How well Banér used this respite was shown a year later when he marched into Bohemia, defeated its army, invaded Bavaria, and almost captured the emperor himself.

This period saw the establishment of the first Swedish colony in America. On March 1, 1638, a large party of Swedes, who had crossed the ocean under the command of the celebrated Peter Minuit, took possession of land on the banks of the Delaware River. They called their settlement (on the site that later became Wilmington) Fort Christina, after their royal princess, and the colony which they were founding New Sweden. The first Lutheran congregation in America was established here by the Reverend Reorus Porkillus and five years later the colonists from Delaware pushed into what is now Pennsylvania, where they founded the settlement of Upland, on the site where Chester now stands. Among the gifts these first Swedish colonists brought to America were the log cabin and the steam bath. The new colony, which never numbered more than two hundred Swedes, did not long survive. In 1655 it was attacked and captured by the Dutch, who incorporated New Sweden into what was then New Netherland.

While all these great events were taking place, Christian IV of Denmark had kept a low profile mindful of his own disastrous attempt to flout the Holy Roman Empire. Christian was, however, bitterly envious of Gustavus' success and he feared that Sweden's occupation of new territories on the borders of Denmark might lead to the encirclement and strangulation of his kingdom. He offered to act as mediator between Sweden and the emperor, but the Swedish Council mistrusted Christian. In the summer of 1643 Lennart Torstensson, who had become Swedish commander-in-chief after Banér's death in 1641, was recalled from a successful campaign in the east and ordered to march on Denmark from the south, while another Swedish army invaded Skåne. Torstensson crossed the Danish frontier in December, 1643, and quickly occupied the whole of Jutland, while Louis De Geer's army, based in Stockholm, seized Skåne.

This two-pronged attack took the Danes by surprise, but Christian IV, now an old man of sixty-seven, rose to the occasion. The king was tireless in organizing his navy and in raising forces, and the next April the Danish fleet met and defeated the Dutch navy, which was preparing to carry Torstensson's troops from Jutland to the islands of Fyn and Zealand. The beaten Dutch sailed back to Holland, but in June a Swedish fleet of forty sail appeared in the western Baltic. Christian engaged the enemy in a ten-hour battle in which he lost an eye and was wounded in thirteen places, but he insisted upon remaining on the deck of his flagship until at last the Swedish fleet was forced to take refuge in Kiel Bay, where the victorious Danes sought unsuccessfully to blockade it.

The Swedish ships escaped from Kiel and combined with the Dutch to attack the Danes near the island of Lolland. In this battle the Danes, who were outnumbered by two to one, lost fifteen of their seventeen ships by sinking or capture, and Christian was forced to sue for peace. By a treaty signed at Brömsebro, on the Swedish-Danish frontier in August, 1645, Denmark was obliged to surrender Jämtland and Herjedalen, Gotland and the island of Ösel, which commands the Gulf of Riga. As a guarantee for the exemption of Swedish shipping from Danish tolls, Sweden also took possession of the province of Halland, which faces Jutland across the Kattegat, for a period of thirty years. An exhausted and harassed man, Christian died in 1648.

Queen Christina of Sweden had by now come of age, and she had been crowned in December, 1644. This handsome girl had a mind even more brilliant than that of her great father, and she had been given according to her father's wishes a man's education under Oxenstierna's direction. The queen possessed one of the finest libraries in Europe, and scholars from all parts of the Continent—René Descartes among them—flocked to her court and were supported by her bounty. Christina was a daring and tireless horsewoman and was inclined to wear male clothes. Her own sex she despised and she regarded marriage as no better than slavery, since it would have brought her under the domination of a man.

Christina became resentful of Axel Oxenstierna's tutelage, and she loathed her chancellor's insistence on routine and punctual attendance to state business. She dreamed always of life in a climate sunnier and warmer than that of Sweden and of the ancient cultures of Greece and

OVERLEAF: *A 1700 painting shows Queen Christina (seated at the table, right) surrounded by scholars and other luminaries at the French court.*

Rome which appealed to her so strongly. As time went on, her neglect of official affairs, and in particular of the national finances, which suffered under her lavish habits, became a grave problem. The looseness of the queen's sex life was another cause of scandal.

It need hardly be said that the queen did not lack for suitors, chief among them her cousin, Charles, son of the count palatine of Zweibrücken and Gustavus Adolphus' sister Catherine. Christina refused all offers of marriage. Nevertheless, dedicated to continuing the Vasa dynasty on the Swedish throne, in 1648 she appointed Charles commander-in-chief of the Swedish army and, a year later, proclaimed him her heir and eventual successor.

The Thirty Years' War was now an intermittent conflict which proceeded by fits and starts. Peace negotiations had begun as early as 1642, but they dragged on in a manner which will be familiar to all who have watched the "progress" of a modern disarmament conference. Only in October, 1648, was the Peace of Westphalia at last signed. Sweden emerged triumphant from the war. She received under the peace treaty large areas of North Germany; she held the mouths of the rivers Oder, Elbe, and Weser; she was paid an indemnity of five million rix-dollars; and, with France, she stood as guarantor of the civil and religious liberties of all German Protestants.

The year that was marked by the Peace of Westphalia also saw the death of old Christian IV of Denmark and the election of his son to succeed him as Frederick III.

Sweden now entered upon a period of glory which has left us, for our enjoyment today, many of the splendid mansions which still adorn the country. Swedish officers returned from the wars laden with plunder and many of them invested their riches in land and in the building of great houses. Such houses include Skokloster, seat of the Wrangel family, on Lake Mälaren; Venngarn and Karlberg, both built by Magnus de la Gardie; Stjärnorp, the home of the Douglas clan, who had done better in their adopted country than in their native Scotland; and in Stockholm itself, Hässelby, the town house of the great Bonde family. Many of these splendid mansions were the work of foreign architects, notably the Frenchman Jean de la Vallée and the German Nicodemus Tessin, who, between 1662 and 1686, built the lovely royal palace of Drottningholm, near Stockholm.

Christina's behavior nevertheless cast a shadow over this bright scene of progress and prosperity. The queen spent money recklessly on the favorites whom she took to her bed, and deeply offended many of the old nobility by showering titles upon these newcomers. During Christina's comparatively short reign the number of Swedish counts was increased from three to twenty and of barons from seven to thirty-four. The queen mortgaged or gave away royal properties wholesale, and her distaste for official duties became so marked that it was impossible to persuade her to attend to them.

By 1654 the situation had become intolerable. Christina's unpopularity, which had been steadily growing among all classes of society, had reached such a pitch that her successor, Charles, prudently withdrew to the island of Öland, opposite Kalmar, in order not to become involved in the queen's affairs. At last, on June 6, 1654, Christina abdicated, against the advice of her council but to the relief of most Swedes. She claimed to approach the day calmly: "I am not in the least anxious about the final applause. I know that the scene I have to perform is not composed according to the laws of the theatre. It is a lot to ask that what is strong, manly, and powerful should win acceptance. . . ." Her cousin was crowned as Charles X on the same day, and Christina, disguised as a male courtier, immediately set off for the south. She arrived in Rome eighteen months later, having publicly proclaimed her conversion to the Roman Catholic Church en route. She died there in 1689 at the age of sixty-three.

Charles X Gustavus, as the new king was styled, was an experienced soldier who had served in the Thirty Years' War. He found Sweden almost bankrupted by Christina's mismanagement, and one of his first acts as king was to investigate the reckless dissipation of crown property which she had brought about. Christina's favorites, who had received large grants of land from their mistress, reluctantly agreed to restore about a quarter of their gains to the king.

Charles decided, as have many rulers before and since, that a war was the best way of distracting public attention from troubles on the home front. He persuaded his council that a war against Poland was necessary, and in July, 1655, he set out for Poland with fifty thousand men and a fleet of fifty ships. At first all went well with the Swedish invaders. They had soon occupied Warsaw. The fortress of Cracow fell after a siege of two months and King John II Casimir took refuge in Silesia. But as winter drew on, the Swedish army found itself checked by the tiny monastery-fortress of Częstochowa. A few score monks and soldiers held out against the Swedish besiegers for seventy days, a feat which in Poland is ascribed to miraculous intervention, and at last the embattled Swedes were forced to withdraw.

The "Miracle of Częstochowa" had extremely unfortunate effects for the Swedes. News of it spread through Poland like a brush fire and kindled the Poles' patriotism. King John Casimir returned to his country, and Polish levies and guerrillas harassed the Swedes everywhere. Warsaw was regained by the Poles only to be recaptured once again by the Swedes and Brandenburgers. But still King Charles' situation was not a happy one; the spirit of the Poles remained unbroken.

Charles was rescued from this awkward position by Denmark's usual eagerness to turn Sweden's difficulties to her own advantage. In June, 1657, Frederick III declared war on Sweden and Charles was able to withdraw from Poland with honor and engage the new enemy. His Swedish force of eight thousand veterans quickly invaded Holstein and dispersed the Danish defenders. Winter set in with a severity unusual even in that part of the world, and Charles, hitherto prevented by the Danish navy from crossing to the islands which must be conquered if the war was to be won, seized the opportunity offered by the frozen channels.

On January 30, 1658, the ice was pronounced strong enough to bear the Swedish army, which then set out across the Little Belt strait to the island of Fyn. Although two companies of Swedish troops sank through the ice during the crossing, the bulk of the army reached Fyn safely and Charles quickly occupied the island. The next step was to cross the Great Belt to the island of Zealand, on which Copenhagen stands, and although his generals advised him against the attempt Charles decided to risk it. "Now," the king said grimly, "we shall talk together in Swedish, brother Frederick."

The march began on the night of February 5, and by the following afternoon the Swedes had reached the small island of Lolland. The French ambassador, who was with Charles' army—diplomats led active lives in those days—described the march: "It was a horror to walk at night across the frozen sea. The horses' tramping had thawed the snow

This carved lion rampant once adorned the warship Vasa *which sank near the mouth of Stockholm harbor in 1628 while on her maiden voyage.*

so that the water rose one or two feet on the ice; every moment we feared to find the sea open somewhere to engulf us." On February 11 Charles and his army landed on Zealand, having executed, thanks to the weather, a brilliant military stroke. The medal which Charles had struck to commemorate the event bears the inscription *Naturae hoc debuit uni*—"This was owed to Nature alone," and this is no exaggeration. The Danish aristocracy, having grown in power and affluence in the preceding century, had seemingly lost their ancient warrior skills. Elaborate and luxurious estates—based upon large-scale farming—had replaced the fortresses of old. And the peasantry, increasingly burdened by the nobility, had become estranged and hostile. When the Swedes invaded, the nobility panicked and the peasantry refused to fight in their behalf. Charles X's attack was to prove the beginning of the end of the Danish aristocracy's privileged position in Denmark.

Now forced to sue for peace, Denmark ceded Skåne, Halland, Blekinge, Bohuslän, and some lesser territories to Sweden before the two kings sat down to a three-day banquet at Roskilde.

Charles soon repented of what he regarded as his liberality to Denmark and wished that he had annexed the country; when the Dutch fleet came to support the Poles and Germans against Sweden, the Danes failed to join Sweden in blockading the Baltic. Charles promptly led an army into Zealand without bothering to declare war. Swedish forces invested Kronborg Castle at Helsingör, and Copenhagen prepared for a siege. The Dutch, whose powerful fleet lay ready to intervene on the Danish side, now went into action against the Swedish navy and drove it back to Landskrona, while Charles encamped with his forces ten miles from Copenhagen.

Once again Charles tried to make ice his ally. The freezing of the sea-lanes had now immobilized the Dutch fleet, and Charles resolved to take advantage of this fact by storming Copenhagen. Frederick, declaring bravely, "I want to die in my nest," stood his ground in the capital. He was joined by the city's burghers, who took the opportunity to strike a bargain in their own behalf. They would resist the Danes in return for a charter making Copenhagen a free city for international trade and tax-free transit of goods, and for the granting of those privileges regarding the right to own land which were previously enjoyed only by the nobility. The Charter of Copenhagen was signed on August

10, 1658, and when Charles reached the city's outskirts he was brought
to a standstill by the citizen army. At the same time the Dutch sent a
large fleet to the Danes' rescue and the Poles and Brandenburgers also
went on the march to help. On the night of February 11, 1659, a Swedish force, its members camouflaged in white shirts to blend with the
snow, assaulted the icy ramparts of the city. The Swedes were thrown
back with heavy loss, and when the ice melted they were engaged by
the Dutch, the Poles, and the other reinforcements which were arriving.
They were finally routed the following November.

Undaunted, Charles called the Estates together at Göteborg to raise
men and money for an invasion of Norway, but in February, 1660,
the 37-year-old king was struck down by fever. He died after appoint-
ing a Council of Regency for his four-year-old son, Charles, and advis-
ing Sweden to make peace with her enemies. Sweden took the dying
king's advice, and in April the long struggle between the Catholic and
Protestant branches of the Vasa family was brought to an end by the
Peace of Oliva. John Casimir of Poland renounced his claims to the
throne of Sweden and ceded Latvia to Sweden, and two other treaties
ended the war against Denmark and Russia. Sweden had now established her natural frontiers, which have remained unchanged ever
since, and the people of the Danish provinces which Sweden had
acquired gradually became reconciled to their new masters.

The successful defense of Copenhagen had, as might have been
expected, greatly raised the prestige and authority of King Frederick
III with the peasants and burgesses of Denmark. The king resolved
to take advantage of this situation to strike at his nobles, who refused
to pay taxes to the crown and whose exactions and cruelties had made
them hated by the majority of Danes.

Accordingly, Frederick summoned the Estates to Copenhagen in
September, 1660, and although the nobility protested that they were
being forced to yield "to slaves who ought to keep within their limits"
—which gives a fairly good idea of the spirit in which they had been
dealing with their tenants and workers—they were obliged to submit
to new and heavy taxation. The burgesses and clergy of the realm then
offered Denmark to Frederick as a hereditary monarchy (the king had
hitherto been chosen by election), and when the royal council and
nobility refused to agree to this the gates of Copenhagen were closed

and the citizen-forces, a kind of home guard, were called out to bring the council to its senses. The council and the noblemen gave way to this threat, and on October 13, 1660, King Frederick III became supreme hereditary ruler of Denmark, his power absolute and above all human laws. In return the king promised a new constitution and the Estates dispersed, not to meet again for almost two hundred years. The promised constitution was drawn up in 1665. It gave the king absolute authority in all things, stipulating only that he must be a Lutheran and keep Denmark undivided. The actual terms of this document, known as *Lex Regia,* or the "King's Law," were not made public until after the death of Frederick III in 1670. At the same time an array of civil administrative reforms were made, including the drafting of Denmark's first nationwide civil law code. Writing toward the end of the seventeenth century, the English ambassador, Lord Molesworth, said: "The Danish people hug their chains, the only comfort left them being to see their former oppressors [the nobility] in almost

A 1661 view of Stockholm's medieval fortress-palace of the Three Crowns, where young Christina lived and where, within the moat, she kept her pet lion.

as miserable a condition as themselves, the impoverished nobles being
compelled to grind the faces of the poor tenants for their own sub-
sistence."

In all his dealings with his subjects Frederick had taken the advice
of his royal secretary, Peter Schumacher, a Danish alumnus of Queens
College, Oxford. As a young man Schumacher had witnessed the coronation of Louis XIV of France, and he had been deeply impressed by
the virtues of absolute monarchy, which he now imported into Denmark. On his deathbed in 1670 Frederick told his son, the future
Christian V, to "make a great man of Schumacher, but do it slowly."
Christian complied with this advice to the extent of ennobling Schumacher, henceforth Count Griffenfeld, but in 1676 the king fell out
with his councilor, who opposed a plan for the reconquest of the
Danish provinces which had been lost to Sweden. Count Griffenfeld
was arrested and sentenced to imprisonment for life under the absolute
powers which he had himself given the monarchy. And Christian
looked again toward Denmark's lost territory.

The regency which governed Sweden during the minority of King
Charles XI had had a good deal of success in persuading the people of
the former Danish provinces to look upon themselves as Swedes, and
the foundation of the University of Lund in 1668 did much toward
implanting Swedish culture there. Sweden's foreign policy, however,
was closely linked with that of France, and when Louis XIV declared
war on the Netherlands in 1672, Sweden was forced to support him.
That same year the shy, diffident Charles—poorly prepared for his new
role—reached his majority.

In 1675 the wolves fell upon what they hoped would be an easy
victim. The Holy Roman Emperor, in concert with Denmark and the
Netherlands, declared war on Sweden. German forces attacked the
Swedish possession on the mainland and a Danish army invaded Skåne.
The hitherto unassertive Charles XI now took personal command of a
force which moved against the Danes in Skåne and was encouraged
by gaining some minor successes in the early days of the campaign.
Nevertheless, the Danes, with the help of peasant guerrillas, occupied
Skåne, and the Danish fleet won a victory over the Swedes off Öland
in June, 1676.

With Griffenfeld out of the way Charles was now fortunate in finding the adviser he needed in the person of Johan Gyllenstierna, a member of his council. Gyllenstierna organized Swedish resistance to such good purpose that at the end of 1676 a powerful Swedish army was able to march into Skåne under Charles' command. At the Battle of Lund, on December 4–5, 1676, Charles won a decisive though costly victory, and this was followed by another success at Landskrona, which cleared the Danes out of Skåne and left the guerrillas to suffer the savage revenge which the Swedes inflicted upon them. The Danish navy, however, under Niels Juel, one of Denmark's great heroes, twice beat the Swedes in 1677, and Sweden's German provinces were lost to her forever. But ultimately, Denmark was the greater loser. In 1679 three peace treaties, more or less dictated by Louis XIV of France, brought the war to an end on terms which were not unfavorable to Sweden, and Charles XI married the Danish princess Ulrika Eleonora as an earnest of good intentions.

In the following year, Gyllenstierna died. By now, Charles stood in no need of advice. His character had been strengthened by war and by adversity and he now governed Sweden firmly and competently. Orderly rule and a generally enlightened administration of Skåne and the other annexed territories hastened the unification of the nation. He called upon the members of his Council of Regency to account for their financial dealings during his minority, dealings which had resulted in the loss to the crown of much money and property. The Estates declared that the king had power to restore to the state property illegally taken in the past and that he might act without the authority of the council if he saw fit to do so. This ended the power of the council, which henceforward became little more than an aristocratic club, and the former regents were put on trial for misappropriation of state funds. It was the judgment of the Commission of State, which tried them, that the regents had been careless rather than criminal, but they were required to refund vast sums to the crown. As had happened earlier in Denmark, the power of the old nobility was severely curtailed to the greater glory of the monarch. The Estates declared that Charles was "an absolute, all-commanding, and omnipotent sovereign King who is responsible to no one on earth but has the power and right to direct and rule his kingdom according to his own desires and as a Christian King."

After this verdict, most of the aristocracy retired, hurt and resentful, to their country estates. But their property was no more inviolable than other privileges—the royal holdings, which had been negligible, now swelled to more than a third of the country, all through appropriation (*"reduktion"*) from the nobility. Although in some ways this may have been to the benefit of Sweden, it had one unfortunate effect. The tradition of service to the state, which the nobles had accepted as a matter of course, was now ended, and this was to prove a loss which was not easily overcome.

Charles XI proved himself a ruler of orderly, economical habits. He constantly undertook long tours of inspection through his kingdom, riding with only a few attendants and unrecognized by most of his subjects, as was his wish. Nevertheless, people in the know learned to fear the appearance of a horseman wrapped in a long, gray cloak, for his arrival meant a searching audit of accounts and a barrage of sharp, well-informed questions. Toward the end of his reign the king was almost always accompanied on these expeditions by his son Charles, who had been born in 1682.

Economical though Charles XI was, he was ready to spend money in the public interest. He raised a standing army of thirty-eight thousand men, built the great naval arsenal at Karlskrona, which is still the chief base of the Swedish navy, and gave Sweden a fleet of forty-three new men-of-war. The king died of cancer in April, 1697, and his fifteen-year-old son ascended the throne as Charles XII.

CHAPTER VII

EIGHTEENTH-CENTURY ENLIGHTENMENT

S amuel Johnson, that celebrated wit, gossip, and man of letters, was to say of Sweden's king: "Were Socrates and Charles the Twelfth [of Sweden] both present in any company, and Socrates to say, 'Follow me and hear a lecture in Philosophy,' and Charles, laying his hand on his sword, to say, 'Follow me and dethrone the Tsar,' a man would be ashamed to follow Socrates. . . . The profession of soldiers and sailors has the dignity of danger. Mankind reverence those who have got over fear, which is so general a weakness."

This comment shows the reputation that Charles achieved in Europe at the height of his fame. The boy who now assumed the crown of Sweden had been well schooled by his meticulous father. Those long tours of inspection had taught many lessons and Charles had a natural aptitude for languages and mathematics. From his father he had inherited a stubborn will, tireless energy, and self-sufficiency; from his Danish mother, a gentleness of disposition which seemed to be at variance with his other qualities but which blended with them very well.

When the Estates met in the fall of 1697 for the official funeral of Charles XI, they were so impressed by his son that, young as he was,

Vallö Convent, a beautifully landscaped fourteenth-century estate, has served as a retreat for aged Danish gentlewomen since 1737.

they proposed that the boy should at once be declared to be of age, and he was promptly crowned Charles XII.

Soon Denmark too had a new king. Frederick III died in 1699 and the Danes entered the new century under the rule of Frederick IV. Frederick at twenty-eight was hardly the man to match Charles XII of Sweden. He was badly educated and could not even speak good German, the official court language of Denmark. Only in the arts did the new king show any aptitude. So enchanted was he by the sights of Italy, to which he had traveled, that throughout his reign he did all he could to bring some of the same graces to Copenhagen. Within the limits of his rather sluggish brain and in the time left over from his many amorous adventures, Frederick worked hard for his subjects, and they liked him.

Some mention has already been made of the fact that whereas serfdom had long been abolished in Sweden and Norway it still persisted in Denmark. In 1702 Frederick IV made a typically muddleheaded attempt to remedy the condition of the peasants and in fact made things still worse for them. Under the old system, known as *Vornedskap,* the tenant farmer was irrevocably shackled to his noble landlord. He was obliged to live wherever he was ordered—generally the estate on which he was born—and to carry out whatever tasks his landlord assigned him, and to work on any terms which his master chose to dictate. Nor could he travel outside his parish.

This regime was good for agriculture but miserable for farm workers, and Frederick, with a stroke of the pen and with the best of intentions, decreed that peasants who had served their mandatory six years of military service were free to choose their own place of settlement. At once the peasants left their farms in such numbers that farming virtually ground to a standstill. Fields were unplowed, crops unsown, even the cows unmilked, and food no longer came into the towns and cities. Horrified, Frederick reversed his well-meant decision and decreed the system of *Stavnsbaand,* or villeinage, which was much more severe than anything that had gone before.

Equally ill-advised was Frederick's foreign policy. He chose to celebrate his coronation in a somewhat unfortunate manner: he at once concluded an alliance with Augustus, king of Poland and elector of Saxony, against the duke of Holstein-Gottorp, whose duchy lay on

Denmark's southern border. The Schleswig-Holstein question, about
which there will be more to say in a later chapter, has been a constant
source of strife, and even today many Danes do not think that it is
finally concluded. Frederick decided to settle it by force of arms and to
divide the duchy between Poland and Denmark.

The duke of Holstein-Gottorp was not only heartily anti-Danish—
always a strong recommendation in Swedish eyes—but he was also the
brother-in-law of Charles XII. When the Danes and their new-found
allies invaded the duchy in 1700, Sweden lost no time in coming to its
aid. Charles' troops marched into Zealand, with the help of an Anglo-
Dutch fleet, and quickly forced the Danish king to make peace with
the duke and to recognize his full sovereign rights in his own duchy.

Augustus of Poland—still revered in Saxony as Augustus the Strong
because he reputedly left behind him 316 bastard children—was not
discouraged by this setback. The alliance with Denmark had also included a secret pact with Russia for the partition of Swedish possessions. In August, 1700, Peter the Great of Russia, undismayed by the
swift defeat of his Danish allies, laid siege to the Swedish fortress of
Narva, on the Gulf of Finland. The tsar's army was eighty thousand
strong, and Charles' military advisers strongly opposed any massive
Swedish defense. Brushing their objections aside Charles led ten thousand men to the relief of Narva, through desolate, boggy country. He
reached the beleaguered fortress on November 20, 1700, and at once
attacked the Russian positions. Charles concentrated his assault upon
the weakest place in the Russian lines and broke through, cutting off
the enemy and taking a body of prisoners which far outnumbered the
strength of the entire Swedish army.

The Swedish victory was complete and devastating and Charles followed it up by turning on the Poles in Estonia and Latvia and hustling
them out of both countries. He then advanced into Poland itself, threw
Augustus off the throne in 1702, soundly defeated an army of Poles
and Saxons at Kliszow and "with only a cane in his hand" captured the
strong fortress of Cracow. Charles was now finally embarked on the
twenty-one-year series of battles to maintain Swedish hegemony in the
Baltic. His early victories in the Great Northern War, as it came to be
known, made him incautious. Charles drove Sweden to the brink of
disaster with his ambitiousness.

Next, Charles marched into Saxony, engaging Augustus once more and again defeating him. Augustus was then forced to renounce his claim to the crown of Poland and to abandon the alliance with Russia by the Peace of Altränstad, signed in 1706.

In 1707 Charles set out for Latvia and Ingria, both of which had been overrun by Tsar Peter (Peter's defeat at Narva in 1700 had been the stimulus for a major rebuilding of the Russian army). During the winter of 1707–08 Charles began to advance on Moscow. After a halt at Vilna to await better weather, the Swedish army pushed on toward Smolensk. By now autumn had already begun and, since there was no hope of reaching Moscow before the onset of winter, Charles decided to spend the cold months in the Ukraine and await the reinforcements. The winter of 1708–09 was the coldest in a century. Firewood would not burn in the open air and the Swedes did what they could to warm themselves at fires of straw. Charles' army suffered terribly from the bitter weather. Even wine and spirits froze, birds on the wing fell dead at the feet of the soldiers, and hundreds of men lost their hands, feet, and noses from frostbite. The strength of the Swedish army was reduced to seventeen thousand and the reinforcements, when at last they arrived after a very slow march, were also far fewer than Charles had expected, for they had also lost many men in battle, and many more from cold and disease.

When the cruel winter finally ended, Charles' advance was hampered by spring floods and it was not until May, 1709, that he laid siege to the fortress of Poltava, while Tsar Peter, at the head of fifty thousand men, waited for the enemy on the far bank of the Vorskla River. Charles' luck had run out. In a preliminary skirmish he was badly wounded in the foot and was unable to exercise command. Hearing this good news Peter crossed the Vorskla, and on June 28 the Swedish forces were driven from Poltava with heavy losses, and fourteen thousand Swedes surrendered to the Russians.

Charles himself rode southward with only fifteen hundred men, his purpose to find refuge in friendly Turkish territory. Peter of Russia, having all but annihilated the invaders, was nevertheless unstinting in his admiration for their leader. "I believe," the tsar said, "that from the beginning of the world there has never been so perfect a man and hero as Brother Charles." Nevertheless, Peter's Cossack troops took advan-

This portrait of Charles XII, "Lion of the North," painted by David von Krafft, hangs at Drottningholm Castle, the royal palace outside Stockholm.

tage of the victory to sweep into Finland and put its people to the sword. Famine and pestilence completed the work of the tsar's wild horsemen, and a hundred thousand people, or a quarter of Finland's population, died.

As was only to be expected Sweden's enemies at once sought to profit from the defeat at Poltava. Frederick IV of Denmark renewed his alliance with Saxony and invaded Skåne in November, 1709. Three months later a scratch force of peasants under Count Magnus Stenbock beat the Danes at Hälsingborg and forced them to retreat. Across the Baltic, Tsar Peter captured Vyborg in early summer of 1710 and went on to take the remaining Swedish strongholds in the eastern Baltic toward the end of the year.

By now Charles had reached Turkey and been given a warm welcome. And with the grand vizier of the Ottoman Empire he devised a plan for the undoing of Peter the Great. No sooner had Vyborg fallen to the new Russian leviathan than Peter marched into a southern trap. With an army of 38,000 men, Peter entered Turkish territory only to find himself surrounded on the banks of the Pruth River by 190,000 Turks. Peter had no choice but to make peace at once, and he did so, granting Charles free passage to Sweden, promising to evacuate Poland, and to demolish certain fortifications. Charles, however, did not return to Sweden. Instead he remained in Turkey and once again persuaded the sultan to declare war on Russia. This second war was not a success from the Turkish point of view and the sultan came to feel that the sooner he got rid of his difficult guest the better. Charles' small force was attacked by ten thousand Turks and Charles himself was taken prisoner, though only after the house in which he had his headquarters was burned over his head. Even Charles realized that he had outstayed his welcome in Turkey, and now he impatiently awaited an escort to accompany him home to Sweden.

Indeed, it was high time that the king returned to his own dominions, since things were going badly for Sweden. After his victory at Hälsingborg the gallant Stenbock moved into Pomerania on Charles' orders, aiming to cross Poland and join his king. A strong force of Germans and Danes blocked this plan, however, and Stenbock was forced to withdraw.

Meanwhile, the War of the Spanish Succession (in its simplest terms a struggle between Europe's Hapsburgs and Bourbons over control of rulerless Spain) was now ended and several European rulers felt free to employ their forces for fresh purposes. Prussia and Hannover joined the coalition against Sweden, and the appearance of these new enemies provoked frantic pleas from Stockholm that their king should return and lead his people in the crisis. Charles XII left Turkish soil in September, 1714, accompanied by only two hundred Swedes. In Hungary the king left his escort behind and, disguised as a courier, spurred northward with only two companions. He left Pitesti, on the border of Transylvania, on October 27, and fourteen days later he reached the Baltic port of Stralsund. Charles had not taken off his riding boots for sixteen days and when the time at last came to remove them they had to be cut from his legs.

Stralsund was under siege at this time, but the king's arrival electrified the disheartened defenders of the fortress. Their low spirits were understandable, since Stralsund was invested by a very large international force of Danes, Saxons, Prussians, and Russians. Under Charles' command, however, the garrison and citizens held out for a full year until it became clear even to Charles' stubborn mind that there was no hope of raising the siege. Evading the enemy ships that were blockading Stralsund and braving some of the worst weather that the Baltic could produce, Charles crossed to Sweden in the fall of 1715 and set up his headquarters at Lund.

Ignoring the advice of his council, which remained in Stockholm, Charles XII set himself to organize the defense of Sweden, with the able assistance of Baron Georg Heinrich von Görtz. This diplomatist had been in the service of the duke of Holstein-Gottorp and his clever, unscrupulous brain was just the tool which Charles needed. The king was an uncomplicated, straight-forward man, quite lacking in the diplomatic suppleness which Von Görtz was able to supply, but with Von Görtz at his elbow Charles XII could be doubly formidable.

Sweden's position was indeed desperate. She had lost all her Baltic possessions and she stood alone against the Northern League—Russia, Poland, Saxony, Denmark, Prussia, and Hannover. Since the elector of Hannover had also become King George I of England in 1714, relations between England and Sweden were also strained, although the two countries were not at war. Von Görtz, however, was able to

point out to his master that this coalition was very much less powerful than it might appear to be, since every one of its members was pursuing separate ends. Poland-Saxony, the baron advised, was a negligible enemy, but Russia was dangerous, since Tsar Peter was utterly determined to win the war. The best idea, Von Görtz suggested, would be to play off England against Russia and he planned to support James Stuart, generally known as "the Old Pretender," who in 1715 landed in Scotland in a hopeless attempt to oust George I and regain the crown of England for the Stuarts. The Swedish ambassador to London, deeply involved in the plot, was arrested and George persuaded the Dutch, who were playing host to Von Görtz, to imprison him. Nevertheless, England did not declare war on Sweden and Von Görtz was soon released to continue his intrigues for a Swedish invasion of England.

Now it occurred to Charles XII that Norway, no more than a province of Denmark, was a weak link in the Danish defensive chain, and in 1716 he invaded the country and reached Christiania (present-day Oslo). The Swedish attackers were, however, too weak to maintain themselves, and Charles reluctantly withdrew.

Two years later, in 1718, the Swedes tried again. In the fall of that

Russian ships are shown attacking an inferior Swedish force off Cape Hangö in 1714. With this defeat the Swedes lost control of the eastern Baltic.

year Charles invaded Norway with a force of thirty thousand men. His first objective was the fortress of Fredriksten, near the modern town of Halden, and in besieging this strong place, Charles showed his habitual contempt of danger. As he was peering over a parapet he was hit in the head by a musket ball. (Many have since suggested that the king was in fact murdered by a traitor, but a series of exhumations from the king's tomb in Riddarholms Church, the last of them in 1917, have failed to prove this allegation.)

The death of "the Lion of the North" utterly broke Swedish morale. The rise of Russia had rendered impossible the task of defending the hard-won empire, but for many of the troubles which subsequently beset Sweden Charles XII himself must bear the blame. He had always refused to nominate a successor, declaring casually when the matter was raised that "there is always a head which the Crown will fit." Worshiped as he had been by his soldiers, Charles' loss left them with a deep distrust of absolute monarchy, and their confidence was not restored by the ugly struggle for the Swedish crown which they now witnessed. The chief candidates were Duke Charles Frederick of Holstein-Gottorp, the son of Charles' elder sister; and Ulrika Eleonora, the younger sister of the late king and wife of Prince Frederick of Hesse. Prince Frederick had been in Norway at the time of Charles' death, and he acted promptly. The Swedish army in Norway supported him and in Stockholm his wife persuaded the council to recognize her as queen. The luckless Von Görtz was arrested and later beheaded and Frederick of Hesse, having seen his wife's claims to the throne successfully concluded, was crowned as Frederick I in 1720.

Frederick I was not allowed to mount the throne, however, without making large concessions to his subjects' new aversion to absolute monarchy. A fresh constitution deprived the king of all real power, which was transferred to the state council and the four Estates of the Riksdag (though in actuality the peasant estate gained little if any of the benefits). Even the king's right to nominate members of the council was removed and the Riksdag became, in effect, four separate parliaments, with the house of nobles very much in control through its majority rule in the Committee on Secret Matters, a body which decided issues of war and peace, diplomacy, finance, and other critical policy. Fifty members of the nobility, and twenty-five each from the clergy and bourgeoisie, constituted the committee, which excluded the peasantry on the theory that they were incapable of understanding such weighty matters.

The negotiations in 1720 ended Sweden's war against Denmark, Hannover, and Prussia, but the struggle against Russia continued. The presence in the Baltic of an English fleet raised hopes in Stockholm that this force might come to Sweden's aid, but the English did not intervene while the Russians carried out a series of what would now be called "commando raids" on the Swedish coast. They destroyed five towns and hundreds of villages, and in August, 1721, Sweden was obliged to sign the Treaty of Nystad, which brought the Russian war and the broader Great Northern War to an end. This same year saw the incorporation of Schleswig into Denmark, under British and French guarantees that it should be Danish forever.

This allegorical cartoon of the Treaty of Altrandstädt (1707) shows an enraged pope repulsed by the Protestant King Charles XII of Sweden.

Times had been hard for Denmark, quite apart from the drain imposed upon her by the long war. In 1711 the country had been afflicted by a lethal outbreak of plague; in 1717 floods devastated the western coasts of the kingdom and in 1728 two thirds of the city of Copenhagen was destroyed by fire. Frederick IV may not have been a brilliantly intelligent king but he was a good ruler all the same. He husbanded the resources of his country, reduced the national debt, built many schools and castles, introduced a national postal service, and founded Denmark's first theater.

His death in 1730 gave the Danes good cause for regret; his son, Christian VI, now came to the throne. Christian was as heartily hated by the people as his father had been loved. He was a strikingly ugly man with a harsh, rasping voice which matched his unpleasing features. Brought up by Germans, Christian had married a dull, pious German princess and his court was a gloomy place, dominated by a spirit of melancholy piety which did not suit the natural cheerfulness and ebullience for which the Danes have always been noted. Balls and plays were forbidden at court, and the royal palace was so heavily guarded that the king became virtually inaccessible to his subjects. Frederick's new theater in Copenhagen was closed, and a royal edict made Sunday church-going compulsory for everybody. Failure to attend brought heavy fines or punishment in the stocks which Christian ordered to be set up outside every church in Denmark. The death of Christian VI in 1746 and the succession of his son as Frederick V was welcomed by most Danes.

Meanwhile, in Sweden effective government was exercised by Count Arvid Horn, celebrated as one of Charles XII's most daring generals and, later, as a skillful diplomat. As president of the estate of nobles, Horn decided that war-weary Sweden needed a long period of peace, and he had to choose his allies with some care. In 1727, when Horn began his rule, Europe was divided into two rival camps. England-Hannover and France stood opposed to Austria, Spain, and Russia, and Horn finally linked the fortunes of Sweden with the Anglo-French combination.

For eleven years Horn pursued a pacifist policy, much to the displeasure of a large number of young noblemen who were eager to follow a more aggressive course, an aspiration in which they were supported by many influential businessmen and burgesses. These aggressively minded young men nicknamed Horn's party the "Nightcaps" or more usually the "Caps," in tribute to their sleepy conduct of national affairs, and in consequence came to call themselves the "Hats."

In the 1730s the alliance between England and France broke up, and the French ambassador in Stockholm, well supplied with money, began to intrigue with the Hats. By the payment of large bribes, he managed to organize a campaign of ruthless agitation and abuse aimed at Horn's government. In 1739 Horn was forced to resign and his supporters were expelled from the council. The Hats, generally men of the lesser nobility and the bourgeoisie, took over.

The aim of the Hats was to take revenge on Russia, with French help, and the outbreak of the War of the Austrian Succession in 1741 seemed to give them the opportunity that they sought. Beginning with a tripartite contest for the Austrian inheritance and the invasion of Austria by Frederick the Great of Prussia, it was to draw many European nations into the fray. France, Spain, Bavaria, and Sweden came to Prussia's support, while Britain and Holland joined beleaguered Austria. Separately, Sweden declared war on Russia. The entire conflict, which was fought in many combinations and in many theaters, including the American colonies (where it was known as King George's War), lasted until 1748.

A Swedish army was assembled in Finland, but it was soon shown to be a highly inefficient force. Its officers were politicians, with little idea of military discipline or morale, and they placed most of their hopes on the upheaval that would accompany the coming contest for the Russian throne. As anticipated, Peter the Great's daughter Elizabeth successfully staged a coup, but the support given to her partisans by the Swedish forces was so feeble that the new tsarina did not think it worth any substantial reward. The Russians forced the demoralized Swedes to withdraw completely from Finland and offered to return Finland to Sweden only on condition that the Estates should elect Duke Adolphus of Holstein-Gottorp as crown prince of Sweden. At the Treaty of Åbo, in 1743, Sweden accepted these terms.

Frederick I of Sweden died in 1751 and Adolphus, a complete nonentity, succeeded him. The new king's ineffectiveness was, however, compensated for by the strong character of his wife, Louisa Ulrica, sister of Frederick the Great of Prussia and a woman of ambition and ability. The Hats, in spite of the fiasco of their Russian adventure, were determined to show their contempt for the throne and its Russia-propped occupant. They even had a stamp made which enabled them to append the king's signature to any document which he refused to sign.

This was hardly the conduct to commend itself to Adolphus and Louisa, who had expected the Hats to reassert the royal prerogatives, and they now felt betrayed. They formed a court party to oppose the Hats and by seeking the support of the traditionally royalist peasant estate tried, without success, to defeat them in the Riksdag. An attempt to raise the people of Stockholm against the Hats was no more successful and the noblemen who had formed the court party were either executed or forced to leave Sweden. The king and queen found themselves obliged to make humiliating and abject apologies to the Hats, and Adolphus came within a hairbreadth of being deposed.

In 1756 the colonial wars resumed between France and Britain and

This 1740 faience bowl from Copenhagen is shaped like a bishop's mitre and was used to serve a wine punch called "bishop." The legend reads "Long Live King Christian VI."

the Seven Years' War broke out on the Continent. Britain was in alliance with Prussia while France, old rivalries for the present forgotten, stood by Austria, which was still resisting the onslaught of Frederick of Prussia. The year 1757 brought the royal couple further humiliation. At France's instigation, Sweden entered the fray by declaring war on Prussia, thus pitting the Swedish army against that of Louisa Ulrica's brother, Frederick the Great. The Swedes fought a completely useless little campaign whose only value was the discovery of the virtues of the potato, hitherto unknown in Sweden but long appreciated by Frederick, who fed his armies on this invaluable root.

This futile war was proving a severe drain on Swedish finances and at last in 1762 Queen Louisa had the satisfaction of being begged by the Hats, her troublesome adversaries at home, to intercede with her formidable brother for peace terms. The Hats had little choice in the matter, since inflation now had Sweden in its grip.

Peace was signed with Prussia on generous terms which restored the *status quo* and three years later the Hats were swept from power. The Caps took over the government of the country, abolished the rigid censorship which the Hats had imposed, and turned for support to Russia instead of France.

In the year that marked the end of Sweden's war with Prussia the semi-lunatic Peter III had become "Tsar of All the Russias," and he was also duke of Holstein-Gottorp, that contentious duchy. Peter's first thought was to take revenge on Denmark, the hereditary enemy of the duchy, but by great good fortune from the Danish point of view Peter III was deposed before he had an opportunity to engage them. His estranged wife and successor, Catherine the Great, at once made peace with Denmark. Thus both Sweden and Denmark had been spared great troubles within a space of twenty years by Russia's domestic convulsions.

Frederick V, who now sat on the throne of Denmark, had been brought up by Christian VI in the narrowest tradition of German pietism, but no sooner was the father dead than the son cast off the shackles of his upbringing. Succeeding in 1746, the new king showed very little interest in affairs of state. He was, however, a gay, sociable person, very much to the taste of the Danish people who had suffered enough under his father's dismal regime, and Frederick's reign was a

joyous time for the Danes. The Royal Theater in Copenhagen was re-
opened in 1747, all restrictions on the pleasures of the people were
abolished, and art and intellect flourished.

Before this time it is fair to say that secular literature comparable to
that developing in Europe hardly existed in Scandinavia. Epic tales,
scientific treatises, religious works and the like had been published, but
literature for its own sake was rare.

One of the first writers to remedy this state of affairs was a man who
is claimed as a native son by both Norway and Denmark. Ludvig Holberg was born in Bergen in 1684 and spent his youth there, but fame
and fortune came to him only after he had moved to Copenhagen,
where he spent most of his adult life.

His education prepared him in philosophy and theology by a two-
year sojourn at Oxford, and another brief exile in Paris and Rome left
him thoroughly involved with the spirit of the Enlightenment. Holberg
is chiefly remembered as a writer of satirical comedies for the Danish
stage. Contemporary Norwegians knew little of his work as no theater
existed there at that time, and he has been called deservedly "the Scandinavian Molière." But Holberg also produced a number of scholarly
historical works during the most dour years of Danish pietism when
that stage was also closed. His earliest comic drama—*The Political
Tinker*—was produced at the newly licensed Danish-language theater
in Copenhagen in 1722, and another of his plays celebrated the opening of the Royal Theater after Frederick V's accession. Some twenty-six
of Holberg's dramatic works ultimately found their way into that company's repertoire.

Another literary figure, born a few years before Holberg's death and
no less influential in the Danish cultural revival, was Johannes Ewald,
who is widely regarded as Denmark's most gifted lyricist. Inspired by
the newly evolving Romantic movement—as Holberg had sprung
from the Age of Reason—Ewald represented the other pole of Scandinavian literature. He dug deep into the history and legends of Scandinavia and brought to thousands of readers in Denmark and in the
rest of Europe a new interest in the ancient North. One of Ewald's
poems, "King Christian Stood by the Lofty Mast," was set to music
and became the Danish national anthem.

Three years after the beginning of Frederick's reign, *Berlingske*

Tidende, now one of the world's great newspapers, was founded, and in 1754 the Danish Academy of Arts was established in Copenhagen.

Meanwhile, Frederick left the running of the government in the trust of Count Johann von Bernstorff, a German who never managed to master Danish, but a wise and able minister, who governed Denmark well for twenty years. Bernstorff encouraged Danish commerce, science, and art and the country settled down to a period of peace and prosperity, while the king indulged himself as a great haunter of brothels and a giver of parties, both of which would have appalled his father. When Queen Louisa, his first wife and mother of the heir apparent, died in 1751 Frederick lost no time in marrying Juliana-Marie of Brunswick. She also bore him a son, and then in 1766 Frederick V died, not surprisingly, of cirrhosis of the liver, at the age of forty-two. His place was taken by his first son, seventeen-year-old Christian VII.

The new king was good-looking enough but weak and nervous, shallow and superficial, thanks largely to his education at the hands of his tutor, Count Reventlow. By the time Christian mounted the throne he was already a thoroughgoing libertine. He was a regular frequenter of public houses and taverns, where his appearance was anything but welcome, since he had a habit of smashing up any furniture and glassware in reach. In 1766 Christian married Caroline Matilda, sister of King George III of England, and they were crowned together the following year, but from the first the king hated his wife and treated her with contempt.

During a visit to the French and British courts Christian fell in with a man who was to have a fatal influence upon his destiny. Johann Friedrich von Struensee, a German, got himself appointed court physician to the king of Denmark and soon became indispensable to his master. Struensee was an atheist of thoroughly dissolute habits, but he was, nonetheless, something of a genius. Thirty-one years of age when he attached himself to Christian, he persuaded the king to treat Caroline Matilda with at least some semblance of decency, and the queen was correspondingly grateful. As Christian lapsed into madness, the queen's affection for Struensee increased, and she became his mistress in 1770.

Struensee, sure now of his power, persuaded Christian to dismiss the faithful Count von Bernstorff and himself took over the reins of government, while a trusted friend, Enevold Brandt, was made the king's jailer and ordered to keep everybody away from him. In 1771 Struensee made himself absolute dictator of Denmark, with the queen's support. He was a fervent believer in Rousseau and the New Enlightenment, and with the best of intentions he strove to reform what he regarded as an effete and outmoded system of monarchy. But Struensee had never learned to speak Danish and knew nothing of the Danish mentality or customs. His well-meant attempts to improve the lot of the peasantry foundered and his laws to abolish capital punishment for theft—an extremely advanced notion—and to make legal procedure more democratic met with a very tepid public response.

Struensee's own demise was hastened by his determination to make Denmark a "permissive society," an aim which has now, it seems, been at last achieved. He decreed that adultery and unchastity were no longer criminal offenses, a chapel was converted into a hospital for venereal diseases, nudity was encouraged, and state lotteries and gambling were declared legal.

This was too much for most Danes, and the queen dowager, Juliana-Marie, the stepmother of the now lunatic King Christian, came to the conclusion that she must put a stop to Struensee's "reforms." Taking her own son, Prince Frederick, and the officer commanding the royal guard into her confidence, she arranged that they should burst into the king's bedroom after a masked ball at the palace, on January 17, 1772. The conspirators then forced Christian to sign warrants for the arrest of Struensee, Brandt, and other members of the government and for the imprisonment of Queen Caroline in Kronborg Castle.

Struensee was locked up in chains and brought to trial for *lèse-majesté*. Learning that the queen was also a prisoner he confessed that she had been his mistress, but this availed him nothing. Struensee and Brandt were sentenced to death. First their right hands were lopped off, then they were beheaded, the heads set on poles, and the bodies drawn and quartered. Queen Caroline's fate was less drastic. An Extraordinary Court sentenced her to be divorced and to imprisonment for life, but her brother, George III, intervened and insisted that she be treated "as an English Princess." His demand was granted and an English man-of-war dropped anchor off Helsingör to take away the fallen

queen. She was escorted to Hannover, where she died in May, 1775, at the early age of twenty-three.

In 1771 King Adolphus Frederick of Sweden died suddenly. His place was taken by his twenty-five-year-old son, Gustavus III, whose accession marked the opening of a new era of enlightened absolutism —so revolutionary in character that it is often referred to as the "Gustavian Epoch." Gustavus' appearance was deceptive—his effeminate manners masked a will of iron, great literary and diplomatic ability, and a large appetite for power and popularity. Gustavus had been deeply shamed when, in 1768, his father had abdicated for six days, thanks to the use of that royal stamp which the council kept in reserve to deal with cases of royal obstinacy. The king had declined to sign a financial document, whereupon the council simply stamped it and tried to push it through the treasury. The king abdicated, the treasury refused to accept the stamped document, and the colonel commanding

the royal guard warned the council that he would not answer for the conduct of his troops if the council persisted in defying the king. The council yielded with bad grace and Adolphus Frederick resumed his reign. His son, watching this depressing episode, resolved that such things should not happen again.

Gustavus was in Paris enjoying its brilliant intellectual and court life when news of his father's death reached him. He returned to Stockholm, where he was enthusiastically welcomed. His first action was to attempt a reconciliation between the Hats and the Caps in the interests of national unity. The effort failed and the king made up his mind to overthrow the government by a *coup d'état*. His fellow conspirators were Colonel Magnus Sprengtporten, who was to march upon Stockholm with the army stationed in Finland, and the crown's forester, Johan Kristoffer Toll, who was to bring soldiers from Skåne. Both officers secured the full support of their troops, but the British am-

Abraham Clemetsson of Sweden's Småland province painted this rustic version of the Story of the Magi in 1796.

bassador in Stockholm got wind of the plot and warned the council.

Before the council could arrest the king, as was their intention, Gustavus sent orders to royalist officers to meet him next day, August 19, 1772, in Stockholm's Arsenal Square. At 10 A.M. the king rode into the square, where he was joined by about two hundred officers, and witnessed the ceremony of changing the guard. After the troops had marched past, the king dismounted from his horse, saying in a loud voice: "As all these gentlemen return on foot I may as well do so also." The officers trooped after the king into the guardroom where Gustavus addressed them: "If you will follow me as your forefathers followed Gustavus Vasa and Gustavus I Adolphus, I will venture my lifeblood for the safety and honour of my country."

The young officers acclaimed this sentiment and Gustavus at once sent an officer and thirty men to arrest the council, which was meeting at the palace, and they were tamely locked into the conference room. The governor of Stockholm was also arrested, and Gustavus dictated a new oath of allegiance for the armed forces, which henceforward were to take their orders from no one but the king. He tied a white handkerchief to his arm as the symbol of the royalist cause. In a matter of hours handkerchiefs were fluttering all over Stockholm. Gustavus had won a completely bloodless victory.

Next day heralds were sent out to summon the Estates to a meeting with a warning that any deputy who failed to attend would be regarded as an enemy of his king and country. The frightened deputies were forced to run a gauntlet of guards with fixed bayonets and found that the hall in which they gathered was surrounded by artillery, the gunners standing by their pieces with matches ready for lighting in their hands. The king, crowned and carrying his scepter, faced the crowd and said: "Liberty has been transformed into aristocratic tyranny. Parties are united only in mangling and dishonouring their common fatherland. . . . Rid yourselves of fetters of foreign gold and domestic discord. If honour is dead in your hearts, my blushes ought to make you feel into what contempt the kingdom has been thrown by you. If there be any here present who can deny the truth of what I have said, let him stand up!" Nobody moved, and the king then read aloud the new constitution, which gave him wide powers, before laying his crown aside and leading the Estates in the singing of a *Te Deum* in thanks for their national unity. No harsh reprisals marred the king's triumph.

Whatever mistakes the Caps may have made in their last period of power, their abolition of the censorship and the so-called "Age of Freedom" which followed it had encouraged the rapid development of the arts and sciences in Sweden. The most notable figures in this revival were Anders Celsius, the great astronomer-physicist who invented the centigrade thermometer scale which bears his name, Karl von Linné (Carolus Linnaeus), who has won immortal fame as the father of modern systematic botany, and Emanuel Swedenborg.

Swedenborg began his professional life as a scientist, and his first books, written in Latin, dealt with natural history. But in 1745 his book *Culture and the Love of God* showed that Swedenborg's mind had turned to religion. He resigned his post as assessor of mines to devote himself to spiritual matters. Inclined toward mysticism he wrote a number of works setting forth his views of church doctrine, interpretations which, he asserted, were received by direct revelation from God. After his death in 1772, his sectarians organized the Church of the Niew Jerusalem, or Swedenborgian Church.

When Gustavus came to the throne Sweden's best-loved poet, Karl Mikael Bellmann, was at the height of his career, and a very strange career it was. Bellmann has become a national legend in Sweden, much as his contemporary, Robert Burns, has in Scotland, and the lives of the two men show some interesting similarities. Bellmann's poems, which he set to music and sang to his own lute accompaniment, have defied translation and are virtually unknown outside Sweden, but there they are reverently cherished, especially in his native Stockholm. (A visitor to Bellmannsro, or Bellmann's Rest, in the city's Skansen Park, may dine on a summer evening in the open air while musicians and singers in eighteenth-century costume sing Bellmann's songs to an enraptured audience.)

Bellmann was born in 1740 and he never left the city of his birth except for one brief flight to Norway to escape his creditors. When he was a young man, Stockholm, with a population of 70,000, boasted no fewer than seven hundred taverns and wine-cellars, and Bellmann is reputed to have sampled the wares of every one of them in company with a large gang of friends, mostly middle-class people of artistic leanings, who encouraged him to produce the countless extemporaneous compositions and poems upon which his renown rests. Gustavus III gave the poet an appointment and a salary with no obligation to work, but Bellmann's bohemian habits did not, in the king's view, make him suitable for an invitation to court.

Gustavus III was a self-centered man who lost no chance for pleasure and display. It was said of him that he had a "Janus face," one side of it expressing a stern devotion to duty, the other a love of ease and pleasure. He modeled his court upon that of Versailles and introduced rigid rules of ceremonial, but poets and artists more conventional than Mikael Bellmann were always welcomed there. The king loved acting and the theater; indeed, among all the learned societies founded during his reign, none was more favored than the Swedish Academy, established in 1786 as a forum for belles-lettres.

More significant, perhaps, to Gustavus' subjects and certainly to succeeding generations of Swedes were his other foundations—the Royal Opera, the Royal Ballet, and the little fairy-tale theater at Drottningholm outside Stockholm. This theater had been built in 1766, before Gustavus' accession, but it flowered under the new monarch. It remains unchanged since the days when Gustavus himself devised the transformation scenes for new productions, the wooden seats still labeled with the ranks of the court dignitaries and servants who were allowed to occupy them, the royal box exactly as it was two hundred years ago.

The establishment of the "Golden Age" to which Gustavus aspired cost him a great deal of money, and so did the rebuilding of the system of justice, during which many of the existing judges were found guilty of corruption and dismissed. Sweden's finances were grossly overstrained and the royal family itself was torn by quarrels, chiefly between Gustavus' domineering mother and his wife, Sophia Magdalena of Denmark, whom the king treated with contempt. With his subjects, however, Gustavus was extremely popular.

In 1776 war broke out between Great Britain and her American colonies and Swedish sympathies were strongly on the American side. Many Swedish officers joined the French forces which were sent to North America and others volunteered for the French navy. No sooner had peace negotiations between Britain and America begun than was Sweden among the first countries to sign a treaty of amity and commerce with the United States. In the meantime Sweden kept out of war, joining Denmark and Russia in a League of Armed Neutrality for the protection of shipping against the warships and privateers, British, American, French, and Spanish, which preyed on merchantmen.

Denmark was also indirectly affected by the American Revolution. Maintaining a neutral position, Denmark pressed for freedom of the oceans and exemption from Britain's blockade and seizure policies, and won its point. This small agriculturally productive country found

The painting above depicts the meeting of two powerful eighteenth-century monarchs—Sweden's Gustavus III and Russia's Catherine the Great.

its foreign markets better than ever before and a brief mercantile boom swept Denmark. The bubble burst in 1784 just as Crown Prince Frederick was reaching the end of a miserable childhood. His father, Christian VII, was hopelessly mad, his mother was dead. The prince, an intelligent youth, took a keen interest in national affairs, which he felt were being mismanaged, and in April, 1784, he persuaded his father to appoint him regent and to sign a document dismissing the prime minister. With the help of his new premier, Andreas Peter Bernstorff (nephew of the Bernstorff who had served Frederick V), Prince Frederick initiated a happy period of social and fiscal reform. He steered Denmark safely through the storms which immediately followed the French Revolution, instituting a number of remarkably liberal changes. Foremost perhaps were his reforms on behalf of the peasants. The regency ended in 1808 when Christian died and the prince succeeded him as Frederick VI. But even before this Frederick had abolished almost all vestiges of serfdom (the Stavnsbaand was repealed in 1788) and established a credit bank to enable the newly freed peasants to buy their land. A free trade tariff act and a banking reorganization plan were instituted as liberal spurs to the growth of Denmark's economy. Laws were passed to provide for the welfare of paupers, and Denmark

Above, a simple yet dignified Finnish country church

denounced both the owning and trading of slaves, the first European country to take this enlightened step.

Sweden's Gustavus III was also busily legislating, though in a less idealistic sphere. To remedy the national finances Gustavus imposed, among other things, a ban upon the private distilling of spirits, which henceforth became a royal monopoly. The king's officials were then ordered virtually to force the people to drink schnapps as a contribution to the tax bill, and barrels of liquor were even set up outside churches, so that their congregations could hardly avoid fortifying themselves— and the Exchequer—after Sunday worship. The Estates soon rebelled against this and other forms of taxation, and in 1786 Gustavus dismissed them. Once again a king sought to distract public discontent by starting a war, and in midsummer of 1786 Gustavus III sailed for Finland with a large army in an attack on Russia which he hoped would have the support of Britain and Prussia.

Gustavus' plan was that his fleet should crush the Russian navy and open the path to Saint Petersburg, but the Swedish admirals, much as they tried to obey the king's command, failed in the attempt. In the meantime discontent grew among Finnish separatists and Swedish officers in Finland, who claimed that the king had had no right to declare war, since the Estates had not been consulted. These dissidents united in the Anjala League, which sought to force Gustavus to make peace and to summon the Riksdag, dismissed two years earlier. The king was rescued from a difficult position, as had been Charles X more than a century before, when the Danes came to Russia's aid and attacked Sweden in 1788. On hearing the news of the invasion, Gustavus rejoiced. He could now return to Sweden and rally the nation without the reproach that he had abandoned his army; as the king embarked for home, the Anjala League presented a declaration but Gustavus felt safe in brushing it aside, declaring that he did not treat with rebels.

Gustavus hurried into Dalecarlia, seeking to emulate his ancestor, Gustavus I Vasa, by raising the peasants in the defense of their country. They joined him by the thousands and the king marched out to meet the Danes, who had struck at Sweden from Norway and were besieging Göteborg. The citizens of that seaport, panic-stricken, were on the point of surrender when Gustavus, having ridden two hundred and fifty miles in forty-eight hours, arrived alone at the gates of the city.

His presence served to rally the fainthearted Göteborgers long enough to allow the reinforcements from Dalecarlia to arrive, and the city held out. The British ambassador in Copenhagen, Sir Hugh Elliot, prevailed upon the Danes to agree to an armistice, and their forces left Sweden in November, 1788.

In the following year Gustavus III again convoked the Estates. The three Lower Estates—the clergy, burgesses, and peasants—were filled with admiration for the king's courage and patriotism, but three quarters of the members of the House of Nobles were either members of the Anjala League or in sympathy with them, and they blocked the passage of the vote for supplies which the king demanded. Gustavus, therefore, pushed through a new constitutional amendment, the Act of Union and Security, which gave the king full powers in peace and war and absolute control over foreign affairs. Twenty-one members of the House of Nobles were arrested, but their colleagues continued to oppose the king, who promptly overrode them and earned their undying hatred. In May, 1789, the council was abolished and all the members of the Anjala League were arrested, all but one of them being pardoned subsequently.

Meanwhile, the war with Russia continued. Russian troops were thrice defeated in Finland, and the war at sea, while not decisive, went in Sweden's favor. On July 3, 1790, the Battle of Svenskund gave the Swedes the resounding victory which they had been seeking. Fifty-five Russian ships were sunk or captured and Russia lost nearly fourteen thousand men counting all those killed, wounded, or taken prisoner. Soon after, the Peace of Värälä ended the war, raising the possibility of a Swedish-Russian alliance in the bargain.

The French Revolution had shocked all Europe, and none more than Gustavus III, with his profound respect for French manners and traditions and for the French court. He proposed to Catherine the Great of Russia that he should land in Normandy with a Russo-Swedish army, march on Paris, and overthrow the Jacobins. The tsarina thought well of this plan and Gustavus managed to sell the idea to the Riksdag. A number of young Swedish noblemen, however, bitterly detesting the king as they did, managed to persuade themselves that their cause was identical with that of Revolutionary France, whose slogan of liberty, equality, and fraternity had made a great impact upon romantic young men all over Europe, and they entered into a conspiracy against Gustavus in which they were joined by many who had private grudges against the king. At midnight on March 16, 1792, during a fancy-dress masked ball at the Stockholm Opera House, Gustavus III was shot in the back by a young aristocrat named J. J. Anckarström. Gustavus did not die at once, and during the twelve days of life which remained to him he begged that his assassins should not suffer for their crime. His pleas went unheeded. Anckarström was whipped through the streets of Stockholm, exposed in the pillory for three days, where he suffered the vengeance of the mob, deprived of his right hand, and, at last, beheaded, drawn, and quartered. Sixty-seven years later the great Italian composer, Giuseppe Verdi, decided that this dramatic murder would make a splendid theme for an opera. He called this work *The Masked Ball* (*Un Ballo in Maschera*). Because of the sensitivities of European royalty Verdi ultimately made a number of ludicrous alterations to historical fact. The opera was set in colonial Boston. Gustavus III, accordingly, became "Riccardo, Earl of Warwick, Governor of Massachusetts," Anckarström was transformed into "Renato," his secretary, and his fellow-plotters bore such unaristocratic names as "Samuel" and "Tom."

CHAPTER VIII

JOINING THE CONTINENTAL SYSTEM

Gustavus III was succeeded on the Swedish throne by his thirteen-year-old son, Gustavus IV Adolphus. The revolution sought by
Anckarström's group never materialized, and for the first four years
of the boy's reign regency rule was nominally exercised by his uncle,
Duke Charles. The real power, however, lay in the hands of Charles'
ambitious friend Baron Reuterholm. This man styled himself a disciple
of the New Enlightenment, a follower of Rousseau, and on excellent
terms with Revolutionary France. But during his four-year stint his
lust for power transformed him into a despot. Under his influence all
courtiers who had supported Gustavus III were sent away from court
in disgrace, and they retaliated by conspiring with Russia against the
government.

Sweden attempted to placate Catherine the Great (alarmed by
Sweden's apparent drift toward Jacobinism) by arranging a marriage
between Gustavus IV and Catherine's granddaughter Alexandra. The
young king traveled to Saint Petersburg and all arrangements for the
wedding were complete when Catherine, at the last moment, insisted
that Gustavus should make concessions to the Greek Orthodox Church

*This cathedral and complex of public buildings was erected in Helsinki in the
early 1800s, bearing witness to a growing national consciousness.*

by allowing it a firm foothold in Sweden. Gustavus refused absolutely, broke off the engagement, much to the satisfaction of his subjects, and Catherine's sudden death probably saved Sweden from another war with Russia.

The king, who came of age in November, 1796, was a pedantic, orderly young man, extremely hard-working, but inexperienced and nervous. His first action on assuming full powers was to dismiss Reuterholm, whose republican ideas he abhorred, and to recall the Gustavian nobles to his court. By now the portentous figure of Napoleon Bonaparte was already casting its shadow over Europe, and most of Gustavus' courtiers had lost all sympathy with France. Many young men of all classes, however, were still fascinated, at a safe distance, by French political ideas, and Swedish presses poured out a flood of revolutionary propaganda until Gustavus imposed a strict censorship, which was much resented.

The last month of 1800 saw Russia, Sweden, Denmark, and Prussia once more united in the League of Armed Neutrality, and the British, determined to enforce their blockade on Continental ports, reacted swiftly. In January, 1801, Great Britain laid an absolute embargo on all Danish and Norwegian ships and soon dispatched a fleet of 53 sail, including 20 ships of the line, to the Baltic under the command of Admiral Sir Hyde Parker, with Admiral Horatio Nelson as second-in-command. The British fleet passed through the Sound (Öresund) unperturbed by the guns of Helsingör, and on April 2, 1801, Nelson, with thirty-five ships, attacked the Danish fleet, which included a large number of floating batteries and gunboats, in the port of Copenhagen. The port was sturdily defended, though the Danish forces were made up largely of raw recruits and students, and Nelson, experienced as he was in such matters, later declared that it was the hottest fight that he had ever known.

After a battle lasting five hours, during which three of his men-of-war were driven aground, Nelson sent a letter to Crown Prince Frederick addressed "To the Brothers of Englishmen, the Danes" and giving notice that unless the Danes ceased to resist he would set fire to all captured floating batteries and their crews. The Danes agreed to a 24-hour truce, having suffered heavy casualties. In this battle eighteen-year-old Peder Willemoes won undying fame. For four hours a gunboat under his command engaged Nelson's flagship, losing eighty of its 120-man crew. Filled with admiration for such courage and determination, Nelson told the crown prince that he should promote Willemoes to admiral. On April 9, 1801, a three-month armistice was signed.

Meanwhile, the murder of Tsar Paul of Russia brought to the throne Alexander I, who had married Gustavus' sister-in-law. The new tsar lost no time in persuading the Swedish king to join the Anglo-Russian alliance against France. This Gustavus was the more willing to do, since he was certain that Napoleon was Antichrist in person. Gustavus declared war on France. *Le Moniteur,* part of the controlled French press, mocked, "Gustavus IV is a weakling who has inherited nothing from Charles XII but his folly and his boots!" An army of thirteen thousand Swedes invaded Pomerania in 1805, but a quarrel with the king of Prussia ended all hope of effective operations, and when, in 1806, Napoleon crushed Prussia, Sweden did nothing to help her supposed ally. In 1807 France occupied Pomerania and the Swedish army retired humbly to Rügen, whence it sailed home without having fired more than a few shots during the whole campaign.

By the secret terms of the Treaty of Tilsit, in July, 1807, France and Russia agreed that, should England refuse to meet their peace terms, they would force Austria, Denmark, Sweden, and Portugal to close their ports to British shipping and to declare war on Great Britain, thus completing Napoleon's Continental blockade. If Sweden, still at war with France, resisted pressure, then Denmark was to be induced to make war on its northern neighbor. Denmark's regent, Crown Prince Frederick, would probably have refused these demands had word reached him, but he was with the Danish army at Kiel, guarding the southern frontier of his kingdom, and remained unaware of the Franco-Russian bargain.

The British at once took preventative action and sent to the Baltic a fleet of 25 ships of the line, 40 frigates, and 377 transports, carrying 30,000 troops under the command of Lord Cathcart, who had, as his second-in-command, General Sir Arthur Wellesley, later to become famous as the duke of Wellington. The fleet entered the Sound early in August, 1807, and the Danes were offered the choice of an alliance with Britain against Napoleon or war, with eight days in which to make up their minds. Since nothing could be done without the assent of the regent in Kiel, and it was not possible to obtain this within the time allowed, the British fleet without further ado blockaded the island of Zealand and laid siege to Copenhagen. The city, with an untrained garrison, was in little shape to resist, and after a three-day bombardment it sued for peace and two days later on September 7 surrendered its fleet. The British then seized all Danish warships and naval stores and carried them back to England. A British garrison was left on the island of Anholt, in the middle of the Kattegat, and remained there until 1814.

The crown prince, naturally furious at this disaster, formed an alliance with Napoleon at the end of October, 1807, and five days later Britain declared war on Denmark. A Franco-Spanish army commanded by one of Napoleon's most esteemed marshals, Jean Baptiste Bernadotte, prince of Pontecorvo, moved into Jutland and Fyn with the intention of invading Skåne, but the combined Swedish and British fleets prevented this force from crossing to Zealand. The sight of this foreign army, however, so terrified poor, mad Christian VII, who had been living in Holstein, that his mind could not survive the shock. He died at last in March, 1808, and was succeeded by the regent as Frederick VI.

Sweden's only ally now was Great Britain, and a force of ten thousand British soldiers was sent to Göteborg under the celebrated general Sir John Moore. However, after a stay of only two months in Sweden, Moore quarreled with Gustavus IV and took his troops home in disgust.

Alexander I of Russia, now very much Napoleon's ally, had in the meantime invaded Finland in February, 1808, and the Swedish forces, about 20,000 strong, hastily evacuated the whole southern part of the country without firing a shot. By May the great fortress of Sveaborg, with a garrison of 6,000 men and mounting 2,000 guns, had surrendered abjectly. Swedish shame would have been complete but for the feat of General Adlercreutz, who skillfully withdrew the army of Finland by a march during the worst of the Finnish winter and, when summer came, went over successfully to the offensive against the Russian invaders. The reinforcements which Adlercreutz expected from Sweden, however, were quite inadequate and arrived in a haphazard fashion. September brought the surrender of the combined Swedish

This 1805 portrait by Franciscus Josephus Kinsoen depicts Charles Bernadotte, Napoleon's astute marshal who later became king of Sweden.

army and the cession of Finland to Russia. The tsar issued a proclamation guaranteeing the continuation of the Lutheran Church, the honoring of the traditional privileges of the populace, and the convening of the Finnish Diet. The Finns, owing little to the Swedes, accepted their new overlord, and that winter the Estates, meeting at Porvoo, proclaimed Alexander I of Russia grand duke of Finland and swore allegiance to him.

Gustavus IV, quite rightly, bore the chief blame in the eyes of his subjects for the disaster in Finland. Now Russia was preparing a double assault on Sweden, one army advancing from the northeast by road while another came across the Gulf of Bothnia. In Finland, Swedish resistance had been betrayed by treachery and cowardice, and now, with Sweden herself in mortal danger, the national will was sapped by a campaign of vilification against the king. Gustavus, solitary and self-sufficient as he was, had no power to inspire confidence in his people, and his mind, trained in the rigid atmosphere of his father's court, was unable to adapt itself to changing times.

In the winter of 1808–09 all Stockholm hummed with conspiracy and things came to a head when Lt. Colonel Adlersparre, commanding the troops in Värmland, marched on the capital "to save the country." Gustavus made ready to join the army in Skåne to oppose this *coup,* but on March 13, 1809, General Adlercreutz, the hero of the Finnish war, led six other officers into the king's bedroom and forbade Gustavus to travel. The king drew his sword but was quickly disarmed and arrested. He abdicated on March 29, 1809, and went into exile. Under the pseudonym of "Colonel Gustafsson" the fallen king began a wandering life which ended in impoverishment in Switzerland in 1837. His son Gustavus, who styled himself "prince of Vasa," as he was entitled to do, entered the Austrian army and in 1877 died without male heirs. Thus the great house of Vasa came to a sad and unworthy conclusion.

Gustavus' uncle Charles, who had acted as regent during his nephew's minority, was proclaimed Charles XIII of Sweden in May, 1809. He soon made peace with Russia by a treaty which cost Sweden a third of her territory, including all Finland and the Åland Islands, straddling the Gulf of Bothnia, and he severed all relations with Great Britain. In the same year peace was signed with Denmark, and the

following year with France. Pomerania, which had for some time
been under French occupation, was returned to Sweden on condition
that she close her ports to British ships and trade.

Charles XIII had no heirs and Prince Charles Augustus of Holstein
was elected crown prince of Sweden by the Riksdag. When the prince
came to Sweden, early in 1810, he made himself extremely popular,
except with the adherents of the former Gustavus IV; his sudden death
during a military review in Skåne in May of that year, although officially attributed to a stroke, was generally believed to have been the
result of a poison plot by the Gustavians. Those who had brought
about Gustavus' downfall took no pains to contradict these rumors,
and public indignation reached such a pitch that at the prince's state
funeral in June Count Axel von Fersen, the court marshal, was dragged
from his coach and beaten to death by an angry mob. (It was a sad end
for the romantic figure who had served Queen Marie-Antoinette of
France and organized the abortive escape plan for the French royal
family.) The troops lining the route of the funeral procession did not
interfere with this outrage, on secret orders from the government.

Sweden was now without an heir to the throne, and the government
told their ambassador in Paris to ask Napoleon for his advice on a
successor to Charles XIII. A Swedish delegation was sent to Paris. Its
junior member, Baron Carl Otto Mörner, was a young man with a
mind of his own. On his own initiative he contacted the French marshal
Bernadotte, who had won the esteem of the Swedish army by his civilized methods and his good treatment of prisoners. Mörner proposed
that Bernadotte might put himself forward as a candidate for the
Swedish throne. Napoleon refused either to approve or to veto this
project and Bernadotte at last consented to the audacious plan. At first
the Swedish public was shocked at the idea, but on reflection the view
gained ground that Bernadotte must stand high in Napoleon's favor
and that the emperor would therefore help him to recover Finland for
Sweden. At Örebro, on August 21, 1810, Bernadotte was elected crown
prince of Sweden by unanimous vote of the Riksdag. Assuming the
name of Charles John, the Frenchman landed in Sweden in the fall of
that year.

Toward the end of his long and fruitful life, the man who was soon
to become Charles XIV John of Sweden liked to claim that nobody

Above, an early nineteenth-century folk painting by Back Olof Anderson of Dalecarlia illustrates the parable of the "Workers in the Vineyard."

had ever had a career like his, and many will agree with him. Born in 1763 in the most humble circumstances in southwest France, Jean Bernadotte was a private soldier in the French army at the time of the Revolution. He soon won the attention of young General Bonaparte and indeed married the pretty daughter of a Marseilles tavernkeeper, Desirée Clary, whom Napoleon had loved and jilted before marrying Josephine Beauharnais. Bernadotte had risen from the ranks to become a marshal of France and prince of Pontecorvo, and now, as he landed in Sweden at the age of forty-seven, with Desirée and his eleven-year-old son Oscar at his side, a still more remarkable destiny awaited him.

It was soon clear to the new Crown Prince Charles John that the 62-year-old Charles XIII, absorbed in Freemasonry and feeble in character, was not the ruler for Sweden in these difficult times. Bernadotte promptly took over the effective government of the country, with the general approval of the people, but he gravely disappointed the radicals who had supported his election. Charles John, an extremely shrewd man, had doubts as to the stability of Napoleon's empire and he did not mean to stake his future or that of Sweden on its survival. He made a pretense of declaring war on Great Britain, but at the same time privately informed the British that he did not really mean to fight them. In fact not a single shot was fired by either side in this "war," while British and Swedish smugglers, with the tacit approval of the Swedish government, made a mockery of the emperor's Continental System by which he sought to close European markets to British goods.

In January, 1812, Swedish Pomerania was occupied by French forces and Charles John went into action. He had abandoned all idea of the reconquest of Finland and now, in April, 1812, he signed a secret treaty with Russia. Tsar Alexander, once again Napoleon's enemy, agreed to help Sweden acquire Norway from Denmark in return for thirty thousand Swedish troops to reinforce Russia's army in Germany. With Napoleon's armies threatening to overrun all Europe, Sweden's compensations had to be postponed and its entire energies directed toward defeating the French empire.

In the spring of 1813 Charles John and his army landed in Germany. The allies had divided their forces into three armies, of which the northern army was under Charles John's command. At the Battle of Leipzig, which sealed the emperor's fate, only the Swedish artillery took an active part in the engagement, and it seemed to some that the one-time French marshal was showing a distinct reluctance to fight his former countrymen. While there may well have been an element of this in Charles John's behavior, he was also contending with resentments among the Swedes, who were impatient to take Norway and mistrusting of these interim adventures. Charles' cautious use of his troops in Germany made it possible for him to lead an army at full strength against Denmark. The Danes hardly resisted the Swedish invasion, their king Frederick VI lost heart, and in January 14, 1814, Norway was ceded to Sweden as a separate kingdom united to the Swedish crown. Denmark acquired in return Swedish Pomerania, Iceland, the Faroes, and Greenland.

Denmark, dismembered by the loss of Norway, which had been hers for four hundred years, humiliated by the British seizure of her navy, and completely bankrupt, had emerged shattered from the Napoleonic Wars. Frederick VI pleaded at the Congress of Vienna, which sought to restore Europe from the ravages of the long struggle, that Denmark should be granted more lenient treatment, but his efforts failed. Nevertheless he found, on his return to Denmark, that his subjects were eager to show their sympathy with him and rallied loyally behind their king. (The fact that Frederick was the first truly Danish king for many centuries may have had something to do with their forgiveness. Unlike his predecessors he would speak only Danish at court and forced his courtiers to do likewise, abandoning German, which had been the official language for hundreds of years. The king also refused to appoint officials who did not speak Danish.)

Norway, accustomed to centuries of Danish rule, did not take kindly to the deal. Prince Christian Frederick, the Danish viceroy, was very well liked in Norway and the Norwegians elected him king, refusing to recognize the treaty which had handed them over to Sweden. Not only Sweden but Russia and Great Britain threatened Norway with dire consequences if she continued her defiance, but the Norwegians were resolved to fight. Charles John invaded Norway and defeated his new subjects in a campaign which lasted only two weeks but in which the Norwegians fought with great courage. Charles John sought no revenge against Norway. The peace terms called for the abdication of Christian Frederick but established Norway as a "free country," governed by its own constitutional laws, "a free, independent, and indivisible kingdom, united with Sweden under one king." Charles XIII was elected king of Norway with Charles John Bernadotte as his heir, and in August, 1815, the parliaments of both countries—Sweden's Riksdag and Norway's *Storting*—passed laws giving Norway full legal equality but ensuring that Sweden would be the dominant partner in the marriage. This generous Act of Union was, Charles John declared, in "homage to the principles and love of liberty which I have been fortunate enough to find inherent in every Swede. This union between two peoples under the aegis of freedom will confute all envious detractors and prove a monument to human dignity, . . . giving comfort to those who have the cause of humanity at heart."

In 1818 Charles XIII died and the crown prince succeeded him as Charles XIV John. The new king was clear in his mind that Sweden and Norway needed a long period of peace to recover from the losses suffered in war and he was, in fact, the first king of Sweden whose entire reign was unblemished by war. Charles never learned to speak Swedish and had little understanding for Swedish conditions, which, since he came from the Pyrenees, is perhaps not very surprising. He was a suspicious man, always fearful for the future of his dynasty, and he made vain attempts to muzzle the rising power of the press, whose criticism sorely angered him. Among the great works undertaken in the reign of Charles XIV was the opening, in 1832, of one of the world's longest artificial waterways, the Göta Canal, whose 347 miles of canals and 232 miles of lake channels link Stockholm and Göteborg. Passage in one of the comfortable little ships which chug gently through two days of splendid scenery remains a traveler's delight.

The reign of Charles XIV also witnessed two interlinked events whose significance only later became apparent. In 1837 a Scandinavian emigrant to Illinois named Ole Rynning published in Sweden and Norway a book entitled *A True Account of America for the Information and Help of Peasant and Commoner.* The book sold in large numbers and inspired hundreds of families, especially in Norway, with dreams of settling in the New World. A trickle of Scandinavian emigrants began at once to cross the Atlantic—two shiploads had already sailed in 1825 and 1836—but it was only after the ending of the Civil War and the opening of the American West to settlement that Norway was gripped by what became known as "the American Fever."

Anybody who reads the works of Norway's Henrik Ibsen (1828–1906) or sees his plays cannot fail to be depressed by the straitlaced, puritan atmosphere under which his countrymen lived in the nineteenth century. Ibsen himself could not bear the moral climate of his own country and spent much of his adult life abroad. Thousands upon thousands of Norwegians resolved to escape, and between 1865 and 1914, 674,000 of them migrated to the United States—the total exodus from Norway in the century between 1836 and 1935 was 861,000.

Sweden, as was natural, thanks to her larger population, played an even more impressive part than Norway in the making of America. Official figures, which are probably on the low side, show that 950,000 Swedes emigrated to the United States (and to a much lesser degree to Canada) between 1851 and 1910. World War I more or less halted emigration from both countries and the tightening of United States immigration laws in 1924 has since imposed a permanent ceiling on the influx of all foreign-born peoples.

The Scandinavian newcomers settled largely in the states of the Middle West and Northwest, whose climate and landscape reminded them of home. Wisconsin, Illinois, Iowa, Minnesota, Kansas, and the Dakotas were developed, largely thanks to Swedish and Norwegian workers, and Swedish colonies took root also in Maine, Massachusetts, and Nebraska. American visitors to Norway, in particular, will find it difficult to discover a Norwegian family that does *not* have relatives in the United States; and thousands more Norwegians have visited America in the ships of their country's great merchant fleet.

When old King Charles XIV John died in 1844 at the age of eighty-one, the sorrow of all Swedes was deep and genuine. No king of Sweden had lived to so great an age and none had been so successful in giving peace to his subjects. King Oscar I, who now took his father's place, was a cultured man of liberal views. He believed strongly in the virtues of developing trade and industry and he was a fervent supporter of Scandinavian union. The idea received strong impetus from the cultural movement for "Scandinavism," which sought to create a better understanding among the northern nations. This spirit of intellectual collaboration, heartily supported by King Oscar, had a strong following in the universities of Scandinavia, and the king of Sweden felt that

OVERLEAF: *Transplanted Scandinavians pose with some of the fruits of their labors in a Wisconsin corn field, circa 1895.*

he could look forward to the day when Denmark would join Norway and Sweden in a United Scandinavia. These hopes were, as usual, soon shattered.

Europe's "Year of Revolutions"—1848—which did much to hasten the emigration of peoples all over the Continent to America, gave the Scandinavian monarchs some anxiety. King Oscar, who had inherited his father's fears for the future of the Bernadotte line, became more and more conservative in his thinking and clung ever more firmly to the support of Britain and France, upon which Swedish foreign policy was based. Russia disliked this policy and when, in 1855, Tsar Nicholas I brought pressure to bear on Sweden-Norway to adopt a pro-Russian attitude in the Crimean War, Britain and France signed the so-called "November Treaty" by which the two powers guaranteed the integrity of Sweden-Norway.

Mid-century also brought the full impact of the Industrial Revolution to Sweden. Foreign markets for Sweden's almost limitless forestry products opened up and the development of steam-driven sawmills made exploitation commercially profitable. Textiles and iron production also underwent fundamental changes as trade restrictions were eased and technology advanced. The Göta Canal had proved a boon to commerce and communication and now railroads were to pay a significant role in Sweden's further industrialization.

With Oscar's personal support, the first Swedish railroads were planned. The main trunk lines were to be state controlled while the lesser branches were to be financed by private capital. Building did not actually commence until after Oscar's death in 1859, and it was Oscar's son, Charles XV, who shared the people's triumph when the main line traversing the southern Swedish peninsula between the capital and Göteborg was opened in 1862. An observer described the excitement as the king descended at stations along the route. "The people . . . had everywhere assembled in countless numbers to gaze on the splendor. Here and there triumphal arches were erected, at one station in Södermanland there was a salute of cannon. The jubilation was universal and the cheering almost deafening. . . . At Hallsberg the rockets flashed and burning firecrackers crackled in the bushes, so that nowhere was one safe from sparks and flames."

Charles XV had inherited a united realm well on the road toward a prosperity exceeding anything Sweden and Norway had ever known before.

Denmark was not to find the path so smooth. Christian VIII died in January, 1848. At the time of his death the king had been planning a new constitution far more liberal than its predecessors, but his son, who came to the throne as Frederick VII, was at first sight not the man to carry on Christian's schemes. To put it bluntly, Frederick had been a spoiled brat. In 1828 he had married his cousin Wilhelmina. The marriage did not last and in 1841 he married Princess Marianne of Mecklenburg-Strelitz with equally bad results. He was again divorced five years later.

However, Frederick had fallen genuinely in love with a ballet dancer, Louise Rasmussen, and on his accession to the throne his first act was to announce his intention of marrying this simple, charming girl whose association with Frederick had done the new king nothing but good. He was dissuaded from this step for the moment, but in 1850 he bestowed upon Louise the title of Countess Danner and married her in spite of all objections. To Louise must go the credit for a great improvement in Frederick's behavior.

In the spring of 1848, however, the Schleswig-Holstein dispute, which had long been simmering, came once more to the fore. Schleswig's population was 50 per cent Danish, 50 per cent German; that of Holstein entirely German. Frederick VII was required by the basic law of Denmark to keep Schleswig intact as Danish soil, and the Danes living in Schleswig clamored for the free joint constitution for Schleswig and Denmark which Frederick had promised on his accession. Their German neighbors, on the other hand, were all for the incorporation of both Schleswig and Holstein into a single state of the German Confederation, and sought to back up their cause with threats of armed rebellion.

The people of Copenhagen were outraged by this development and, aroused and led by Denmark's Liberal Party leaders, the citizenry marched through the capital to the royal palace to present their demands for the dismissal of the ministers who had allowed matters to deteriorate thus. The king, well aware of the thrones which were at that very moment tottering around him, needed no one to convince him of his next move. He announced that he regarded himself thenceforth as a constitutional monarch and invited the parties to form a coalition government to take over the reins of government. While other European capitals were being drenched in the blood of rebellion Denmark's bourgeoisie had accomplished peacefully the overthrow of absolute monarchy! The king of Prussia was persuaded to take up the case of the German rebels, who had captured the fortress of Rendsburg without difficulty, thanks to the capitulation of its German-speaking defenders. However, the Danish army inflicted a sharp defeat on the rebels near Flensburg, whereupon thirty thousand Prussian and German federal troops invaded Schleswig and on Easter Sunday, April 23, 1848, beat Denmark's smaller army in the hard-fought Battle of Schleswig. Denmark appealed to Great Britain and Russia as co-guarantors of Schleswig with Denmark; both powers protested to Berlin, and Sweden-Norway moved fifteen thousand troops to the island of Fyn, ready to intervene. Under the pressure of Russia's threatening attitude, Berlin withdrew its forces from South Jutland, while the Danish navy blockaded German ports on the Baltic and North seas.

In August, 1848, a seven-month armistice was signed, but so harshly did the Germans in Schleswig treat their Danish neighbors that the war resumed in April, 1849. The German forces reoccupied Schleswig and parts of Jutland and besieged Fredericia, on the narrow strait which separates Jutland and Fyn. By a dashing sortie the garrison overran the German entrenchments around the town, captured all their guns, and took two thousand prisoners. The result of this success was another armistice, under which Schleswig was to be administered by an international commission of Danish, Prussian, and British representatives. Prussian intrigues soon reduced this body to impotence, but, again under Russian pressure, Prussia was obliged in July, 1850, to sign a peace treaty with Denmark restoring matters to their prewar status.

The Germans were not pleased with this result and a rebel force of thirty-three thousand men invaded Schleswig only to be soundly beaten by the Danes. The Peace of Berlin was then enforced and Schleswig was divided into three linguistic districts, one Danish-speaking, one of mixed language, and one German.

The fact that Frederick VII, the last of the Oldenburg dynasty, was childless, was also of international import. The London Conference of 1852 met to determine a successor, and they chose Prince Christian of Schleswig-Holstein-Sönderburg-Glücksborg, who mounted the throne upon Frederick's death in 1863 as Christian IX. He was to steer Denmark through another, more disastrous struggle over Schleswig-Holstein.

Charles XV of Sweden was, like his father, a strong believer in Scandinavian unity and his feelings were extremely anti-German. A kindly, cheerful man, he was an amateur poet, painter, and musician, and if he had had his way Swedish control over Norway would have been greatly relaxed. Swedish public opinion, however, would not allow the king to abolish the office of viceroy in Norway, as he sought to do, nor when a crisis arose would it permit him to go to the aid of Denmark. In the interests of Scandinavian solidarity Charles had personally promised the Danes that Sweden would help them against Prussia and the other German states if necessary, and when, in February, 1864, an Austro-Prussian army of fifty-six thousand men invaded Denmark, Charles sought to make good his word. His ministers, however, refused to support him, as did the Swedish people, traditionally anti-Danish. Sweden watched in silent inactivity the downfall of her neighbor—a fact which the Danes have still by no means forgotten.

The German invaders opposed a poorly equipped Danish army, which was forced to retreat. The fortress of Dybböl held out for two months but was at last stormed and captured with heavy Danish losses. A peace conference in London failed to agree on terms satisfactory to both sides, which is not surprising, since Prince Bismarck, the dominant figure in the Austro-Prussian coalition, would be satisfied with nothing less than the complete annexation of both Schleswig and Holstein. In June, 1864, the Germans crossed the Little Belt in flat-bottomed boats and overwhelmed the Danish garrison on the island of Als, opposite Flensburg. The Austro-Germans occupied Jutland and Denmark sued for peace. Under the treaty signed in Vienna on September 30, 1864, Denmark was forced to yield up Schleswig, Holstein, and the duchy of Lauenburg; the loss represented more than two fifths of her territory and population. Although many Swedish volunteers fought on the Danish side, all hopes of Scandinavian unity were wrecked by this disaster, and the wreck has never been salvaged.

In 1866 Sweden was given the parliamentary system which, basically, she still enjoys. The cumbersome four-house Riksdag became a body of two chambers, the members of the upper chamber elected for nine years by Communal Councils all over Sweden, those of the lower chamber chosen every three years by all voters fulfilling certain property qualifications.

Among the social problems which the new Riksdag had to face was that of alcoholism. After the abolition in 1800 of Gustavus III's royal monopoly over distilling, Sweden was engulfed in what a writer of the time described as "a veritable torrent of liquor." By 1870 every man, woman, and child in Sweden was consuming, on average, no less than ten *gallons* of spirits each year (the present consumption averages about one and a half gallons). A temperance crusade led to the introduction into Sweden and Norway in 1865 of the so-called "Göteborg System." All public houses and taverns were closed and the drinking of spirits was restricted to drams bought in restaurants with meals and consumed on the spot. By the turn of the century average national consumption of liquor had been reduced to two gallons and the following years were to bring still further efforts at reform.

In 1872 Charles XV of Sweden died. His son, Oscar II, who was destined to reign for thirty-nine years, was a man of great culture and knowledge, and his era brought to fruition all the work which had been done in the nineteenth century. Oscar achieved, as his father had never been able to do, the abolition of the office of viceroy in Norway; he reorganized and strengthened the armed forces by introducing conscription and he strove to bring about a new relationship with Norway. Events were to show, however, that the mere abolition of the viceroyalty was not enough for the Norwegians.

Under the prime minister of Norway, Johan Sverdrup, a Liberal, the demand for full equality within the Union became vociferous. Three times between 1874 and 1880 Norway's Storting passed constitutional amendments providing for the seating of members of the Union cabinet at debates of the parliament (whereby the executive and legislative arms of government might work together), and on each occasion Oscar II vetoed them. At the third veto the conflict became bitter and many prominent Norwegians, including the famous poet-patriot Björnstjerne Björnson, spoke during the elections of 1882 in favor of an independent Norwegian republic. The two countries were miles apart in their outlook, history, and economies, and Norwegians could see no advantage to themselves in a lasting political tie with Sweden.

Indeed, while Norway continued to be an essentially farming and seafaring nation, much as it had always been, Sweden had entered the industrial age. In the 1880s and '90s Swedish agriculture ceased to be based on cereals and, under the unbrella of a protectionist policy, the country began to build up an extensive dairy industry and to export its products. With the building of the world's most northerly railroad, the vast iron ore deposits at Gällivare and Kiruna in Norrland were opened up, and the increasing use of electricity enabled Sweden, with her vast reserves of water power, to take full advantage of the latest industrial techniques. She could face the new century with confidence.

Much of the credit for the great advances in the Swedish economy must go to Sweden's inventors. Alfred Nobel, who is now chiefly remembered as the founder of the trust which awards munificent prizes to authors, scientists, and promoters of peace, was the inventor of dynamite. The name of another Swede, L. M. Ericsson, is almost as closely identified with the development of the telephone as is that of Alexander Graham Bell. Primus' stove, Wingquist's ball bearings, and many other Swedish inventions were contributed to Western technology at this time.

No account of Scandinavian history in the nineteenth century, however brief, can close without mention of the artistic and cultural contributions which the four northern nations made during those hundred years. In literature Denmark's Hans Christian Andersen (1805–75) has probably achieved more international fame than any other Scandinavian writer. The Danes have not been slow to take advantage of this, and many visitors to Andersen's hometown of Odense, on Fyn, may feel that the worship of an attractive but second-rate author has been carried too far. The whole town is a museum to a man whose own life was sad and disordered and whose best writings are mostly on themes borrowed from German and Danish folklore.

More influential, though less widely read than Andersen, was and is his fellow countryman Sören Kierkegaard, a philosopher whose writings have greatly affected modern thinking. Kierkegaard, much of whose important work was written during a self-imposed exile in Berlin in the 1840s, was an individualist who revolted against the belief in fellowship and communal action expressed by the widely acclaimed

German philosopher Hegel. The individual personality, Kierkegaard proclaimed, was all-important and organized society was an almost obscene nonsense. Kierkegaard died in 1855 and his works were little read until Georg Brandes, a Danish literary critic with a European reputation, published a study of his philosophy some twenty years after Kierkegaard's death.

In the field of sculpture, too, Denmark produced a controversial figure in the person of Bertel Thorvaldsen, whose ideas of his own genius were unlimited, whatever may be thought of him today. Thorvaldsen, like many artists of his era enamored of classical antiquity, studied in Greece and Italy. He came back to Copenhagen in 1838 determined to give Denmark an infusion of culture. He did what he had set out to do. An extremely skilled craftsman, Thorvaldsen was untiring in producing what has been justly called "a smooth, sentimentalized version of Greece and Rome," as a visit to the Thorvaldsen Museum in Copenhagen will readily confirm. Perhaps his most celebrated work is the "Lion of Lucerne," a Swiss monument dedicated to the Swiss Guards who died protecting the French royal family during the French Revolution.

Meanwhile, in Finland, administrative ties with Sweden had been exchanged for ties with Russia, but literary life such as it was continued to develop in its own fashion. Despite the cross-currents of Classicism, Romanticism, and Realism that were playing elsewhere in Europe, Finland's chief concern in the nineteenth century was the development of a unified national language. Literature and theater could not emerge until a Finnish language had been developed and accepted among cultivated men, who up to that time had been conversant only in Swedish. Finland's vast store of folklore offered the most promising area of exploration to the generation of writers who first tackled the language problem. Writing in 817, a student argued: "No independent nation can exist without a fatherland, and no fatherland can exist without folk poetry [which is] nothing more than the crystal in which a nationality can mirror itself." The key figure in this search for a national identity was Elias Lönnrot, who as a philologist-folklorist, collected materials from the Lapps, the Estonians, the Karelians, and other Finnish tribes, and assembled both the first dictionary of the Finnish language and its first extensive written literature. His legend,

A Finnish beggar, as depicted by the British traveler-artist J. A. Atkinson

Kalevala (1835), a compilation of some twenty-two thousand lines of oral history, tells in epic form the mythic history of the Finns from the Creation to the coming of Christianity, and it served as a rallying point for Finnish nationalist feeling, not only in subsequent literature, but in painting, sculpture, music, and political life, as the people moved toward independence.

Sweden's contributions to literature during this period are best represented by August Strindberg (1849–1912) and Selma Lagerlöf (1858–1940). Strindberg has suffered from his translators, as far as the world outside Scandinavia is concerned; his eminence as a playwright is now universally acknowledged and his plays, despite their acid content, are still popular. But few of his many novels and short stories, excellent as they are, have received abroad the appreciation which they deserve. Strindberg was a down-to-earth, economical writer, intense and disciplined at one moment, explosively bitter at another. Although he was a firm believer in the superiority of the male sex and held strongly that woman's place was in the home, he successively married no fewer than three "career women"—in itself a bold thing to do at that time—and his antifeminist views never prevailed in his own home

No one can say, on the other hand, that Selma Lagerlöf has been ill-served by her translators. Her *Gösta Berling* saga, published in 1891, depicts one momentous year in the life of a rural Värmland community such as she had known in her childhood. This brilliant epic at once established her as a novelist of world stature, and in 1909 she was the first Swedish author to receive a Nobel Prize. Her books and stories, for the most part concerned with the eternal struggle between good and evil, are also paeans to the Swedish countryside and her people.

In addition to Henrik Ibsen, Norway has given the world the great nineteenth-century romantic composer Edvard Grieg (1843–1907). Perhaps best known of all his works is his incidental music to *Peer Gynt,* which he completed in 1875 at Ibsen's request when the latter was director of the theater at Bergen. In his search for a national musical idiom and in his discovery of the richness of native folk music, Grieg launched Norway's modern musical tradition.

A Norwegian playwright more celebrated in his day than Ibsen— he even snatched the Nobel Prize from under Ibsen's nose—was

Björnstjerne Björnson. Björnson probably did more than any other man
to inspire the feelings of patriotism in his fellow countrymen which
were to lead to the independence of Norway early in the twentieth
century. In his plays and poetry Björnson linked Norway's past history
with her modern problems, and whereas Ibsen, hating the atmosphere
of his own country, took refuge abroad, Björnson stayed at home to fan
the fires of freedom. His poem "Yes, we love this land" became the
national anthem.

The greatest single artistic asset to Scandinavia during this century,
in the eyes of the world public, however, was Johanna Maria Lind,
generally known as Jenny Lind, and christened "the Swedish Nightin-
gale." She was born in 1820 in Stockholm, poor and illegitimate, but
by the time she was eighteen her extraordinary voice had already captured her native city. Two years later King Oscar I made the girl his
"chief singer"; she became a member of the Swedish Academy of
Music and, with further training, her natural voice developed a quality
and strength which, it is claimed, has not been equaled since.

Jenny Lind developed a romantic friendship with the great composer Felix Mendelssohn, and after his death, in 1847, she began anew
her career as a concert singer. Her tour of the United States, under the
management of P. T. Barnum, was a triumph, but at last she abandoned
popular concerts in favor of religious music. In 1852 Jenny married
and settled in England, where Queen Victoria was one of her most
ardent admirers. She was extremely charitable, her gifts to good causes
totaling, it is said, $150,000, a vast sum in those days. She became chief
professor of the Royal College of Music in London and died in Mal-
vern at her summer home, in 1887. A plaque to Jenny's memory may
be seen in Westminster Abbey, between the memorials dedicated to
Shakespeare and Byron and just below that of the great Handel. The
fatherless Stockholm slum child had come a long way.

CHAPTER IX

FOUR IN FREEDOM

The dawn of the twentieth century saw, in two of the four Scandinavian nations, a surge of nationalist feeling which was not long to be resisted. Finland had now been Russian for nearly one hundred years and the autocratic rule of the tsar, very different from the Swedish yoke which had rested comparatively lightly upon Finnish shoulders in previous centuries, was chafing and infuriating the people.

Finnish resistance to foreign rule had been most effectively focused in the cultural sphere. Thanks largely to the stimulus of Lönnrot's popularization of the *Kalevala,* interest in the Finnish language was revived among the educated classes, and in 1902 Finnish and Swedish were given complete equality as official languages in Finland.

The year 1865 was the birth of Jean Sibelius, a doctor's son who was destined to become one of the greatest symphonic composers of all time and like Lönnrot a vital force in the regeneration of his native country. Unlike Norway's Greig, Sibelius was inspired only indirectly by Finland's folk music, but he is nevertheless widely regarded as a nationalistic composer because his fame brought attention to his native land. His symphonic poem *En Saga,* inspired by the *Kalevala* and first

In the photo at left, brightly colored houses dot the landscape of Vestmanna, a sheltered fishing hamlet in the Faeroes.

performed in 1892, won him an acclaim which went far beyond Finland's borders; in 1899 the tone poem *Finlandia,* one in a series of "Historical Scenes," drew the West's attention to the plight of a nation-to-be to which most of them had never, until then, given a thought.

Meanwhile, Norway, by no means oppressed by the Swedes, was restive for independence. She found her most eloquent symbol of national vigor in the person of a great explorer and humanitarian. Fridtjof Nansen, born in 1861, startled the world in 1888 by being the first man to cross Greenland on skis. In 1893 he became internationally famous by coming closer to the North Pole than any other man had yet managed to do. Although Nansen's attempt to reach the exact point of the earth's northern extremity failed, he returned home not merely a national hero but enjoying much the same kind of world fame as was to be accorded, thirty-four years later, to Colonel Charles Lindbergh for his first solo air crossing of the Atlantic Ocean.

In 1905 the Norwegian government told the Union government in Stockholm that since Norway had the second largest merchant fleet in the world she was entitled to her own consular service throughout the world and that she was empowered, under the Union Constitution, to establish this service on her own initiative and without reference to Sweden. The Swedes insisted on negotiations, but the Norwegians quickly sabotaged the talks, and set up their consular service. When King Oscar refused to assent to this the Norwegian ministers resigned.

King Oscar declined to accept their resignations, but the Norwegians stood firm, and in June, 1905, they issued a declaration which said: "As King Oscar II has announced that he is unable to form a government in Norway, he has thereby ceased to reign."

This flat assertion, backed as it was by the unanimous vote of the Storting, infuriated the Swedish Riksdag and Swedish opinion generally. The Norwegian people, voting in a plebiscite in August, indicated by 368,208 to 184 that they were ranged no less angrily behind their government. Troops stood by on both sides of the frontier and war seemed imminent when Fridtjof Nansen intervened. Employing all that skill in international negotiation which was so greatly to benefit mankind during the next quarter century, Nansen brought his prestige to bear on obtaining a peaceful solution to the quarrel. Agreement between Sweden and Norway was peaceably reached on September 23,

1905, and approved by King Oscar three days later. Charles, the second son of the Danish crown prince, Frederick, ascended the throne of an independent Norway as King Haakon VII (taking a royal name that went back to medieval times when Norway had been an independent kingdom) and the last attempt at Scandinavian union was ended.

In Finland, meanwhile, events were moving toward a climax. In February, 1899, the Russian tsar pressed his policy of "Russification," by which he hoped to thwart Finnish nationalism. He declared the Finnish constitution henceforth applicable only where it related to local laws. "We have found it necessary to reserve to ourselves the final decision as to which laws come within the scope of general Imperial [Russian] legislation." He refused to accept a petition, signed by 520,000 Finns and delivered to the tsar by a deputation of five hundred Finns, begging him to restore the constitution. The Finnish army was disbanded, Finnish judges dismissed from the bench, and the Russian secret police embarked upon the now familiar program of widespread arrests and imprisonment without trial.

In June, 1904, the Russian governor-general was fatally shot as he was entering the senate house in Helsinki, by a young Finn named Eugen Schauman. The assassin, a member of a distinguished family and son of a former senator, committed suicide immediately after the attack, and he is honored in Finland today as a martyr. The succeeding governor-general, Prince Ivan Obolensky, showed himself a better diplomat than his predecessor. He sought to conciliate, but in October, 1905, the Finns took advantage of the crisis in Russia—a massive general strike which followed the "Bloody Sunday" massacre in Saint Petersburg had wrested the promise of a new constitution from Tsar Nicholas II—to demand a new constitution of their own.

In November, 1905, the tsar granted the Finnish demands. A new constitution replaced Finland's antiquated four-estate assembly with a unicameral Diet of two hundred members, elected every three years by all Finnish men *and women* aged twenty-four and over. The Finnish parliamentary system thus became, at a stroke of the tsar's pen, the most democratic in the world, and twenty-five women were elected to sit in the first Diet to meet under the new dispensation. Universal suffrage instantly raised the voting population from 126,000 male property owners to 1,270,000.

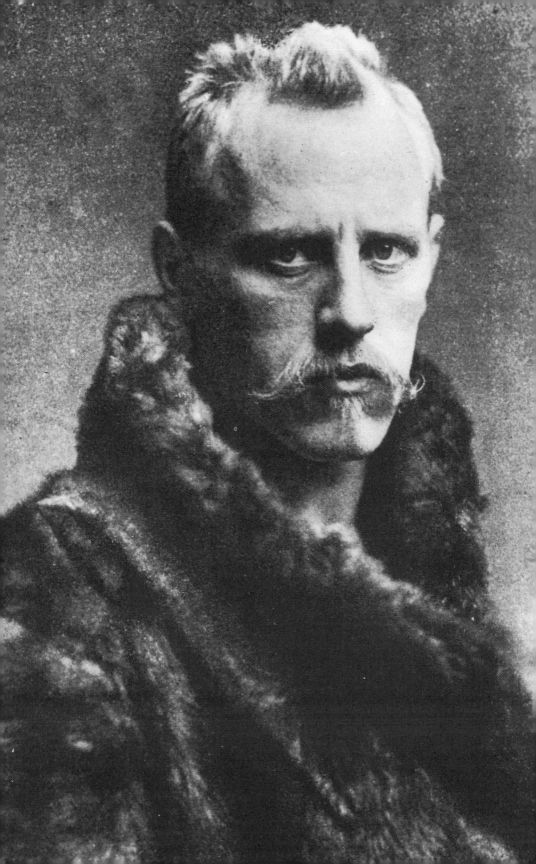

The next few years of parliamentary government were marred by much factionalism, and the tsar found reasons to dissolve the body four times within three years, and to leave unsigned—and thus unimplementable—numbers of laws dealing with political and social reform. In 1910 the Finnish Constitution, so reluctantly granted by Tsar Nicholas less than five years earlier, was arbitrarily abolished by that same short-sighted autocrat. Still more oppressive and humiliating efforts at Russification were imposed, and when World War I broke out neutral Finland was subjected to suspension of civil rights, food rationing, and commercial interference such as a warring Russia found convenient to its own cause. The Finns, relatively compliant for ninety years, now saw their only future in complete secession from Russia. Everything depended on Russia's defeat and the tsar's overthrow.

In January, 1906, the aged Christian IX of Denmark died and his place on the throne was taken by his sixty-three-year-old son Frederick VIII. A year later Oscar II of Sweden also died, brokenhearted by the loss of Norway, and was succeeded by his son Gustaf.

Gustaf V, whose reign was to last until 1950, was a mature man of forty-nine when he ascended the throne. By his marriage to Victoria, the daughter of the grand duke of Baden, in 1881, King Gustaf brought back to the Swedish royal family some of the blood of the Vasas, since Queen Victoria of Sweden was the great-granddaughter of Sophia, daughter of Gustavus IV of Sweden.

King Gustaf V was remarkably tall and lean, a noted tennis player, a great player of bridge. He proved a wise and prudent monarch. He was also a living link with what now seems a remote past. King Gustaf, who had been born in 1858, could recall being tucked into bed and kissed good night as a very small boy by his great-great grandmother. This old lady was the dowager queen Desirée, once betrothed to Napoleon, and first queen-consort of the Bernadotte dynasty.

When Frederick VIII of Denmark died in 1912, to be succeeded by his son as Christian X, the shadows of war were already creeping across Europe, though most people did not yet perceive them. When war came, in August, 1914, Finland, as a Russian grand duchy, was automatically dragged into it. The three free Scandinavian nations were as one in declaring their neutrality, although their sympathies in the conflict were not identical. Sweden, with its strong German con-

This photo of Fridtjof Nansen was taken after an attempt to reach the North Pole in 1896. He later gained fame as a Norwegian diplomat and humanitarian.

nections through the royal family and intermarriage among the upper classes, was, on the whole, pro-German in sentiment. Denmark, still vividly remembering the struggle with Prussia only fifty years before, was firmly, if discreetly, pro-Allies and so was Norway, which was to lose half its merchant navy in the four years of the struggle.

Perhaps the most noteworthy domestic event in Scandinavia during the war years was the granting by Denmark of universal suffrage to all citizens over twenty-five in 1915, thus following Finland's frustrated efforts in the same direction. Another event—important to the United States—was the purchase, in 1917, of the Danish West Indies, parts of which had been occupied by the Danes since 1666. The negotiations for the sale by Denmark had been completed in 1902, but the actual transfer of what are now the Virgin Islands to the American flag was effected at this time.

In March, 1917, the Russian Revolution at last gave Finland the opportunity which she had so long sought. After the Russians revoked the new Finnish constitution in 1910, the country was honeycombed with secret patriotic societies all seeking the freedom of their nation. Some of these groups, organized on military lines, had been trained by German instructors and were in contact with the Russian revolutionaries, who were also supported by the Germans. Within two weeks of the tsarist regime's collapse, the new Russian provisional government cancelled the Russification decrees and reinstituted Finnish self-rule. But disputes within the Finnish government delayed Finland's declaration of independence until the end of the year. The new state was quickly recognized by most of the important powers on both sides of the war, save Great Britain, the United States, and Japan, which hesitated for seventeen months. Nevertheless, the republic of Finland was officially proclaimed on December 6, 1917.

The birth was a painful one. Although all Finns were united in their wish for freedom, they differed radically in their ideas of the kind of freedom they desired. Two factions predominated: the Red Guards, backed by the Russian Bolsheviks and by bodies of Russian troops who had remained in Finland, sought to establish a revolutionary government along Soviet lines, while the Civil (or "White") Guards wished the republic to be governed on more conservative and traditional lines. (A strong royalist faction all but succeeded in instituting a monarchical system of government. Except for their candidate's refusal to take the job, they might well have done so.) The senate appointed a distinguished Finnish officer, Lieutenant-General Gustaf Mannerheim, as commander-in-chief of the Civil Guard, which became the official Finnish army. After a period of terrible bloodshed which lasted for three and a half months, Mannerheim, with German support, crushed the Red Guards and Finland was left to lick her wounds and to build up the underdeveloped economy. The republic's success in doing this in spite of the violent changes of fortune which have afflicted Finland during the past half century is an economic miracle.

Norway was also, at last, heavily concerned with industrial development, which had hitherto passed her by. In 1900 Norwegian industry, such as it was, had used only 200,000 horsepower of energy. With the rapid development of hydro-electric power which followed her independence, this figure had been multiplied sixfold by 1915.

The end of the war in November, 1918, saw the Scandinavian nations united at least in bringing help to Europe's innocent victims. Norway was particularly active in this effort. Many Norwegians reflected bitterly when they were invaded by Hitler's army in 1940 that not a few of the soldiers who shot down Norwegians and, later, swaggered about the streets of Norway's towns and cities were paying a second visit. Their first stay in Norway had been as small children whom Norway had nurtured in the earlier war's aftermath.

Fridtjof Nansen, who had spent the war largely in ensuring that Norway was able to import enough wheat for her essential needs, now led the Norwegian delegation to the first meeting of the League of Nations, upon which Scandinavians, like the rest of mankind, placed such high hopes. He was appointed League High Commissioner for Prisoners of War, his chief concern the German and Austrian prisoners who were starving in Russian captivity. Working with the International Red Cross and the Y.M.C.A., Nansen, by 1922, had arranged for the freedom of 427,000 prisoners of twenty-six nationalities, and it was he who organized the relief measures which did much to alleviate the terrible famine which followed the civil war in Russia. After the Greco-Turkish war of 1922, it was again Nansen who negotiated the exchange of one million Greek prisoners for a half million Turks. Of Nansen's work a British statesman declared: "There is not a country of Europe where wives and mothers have not wept in gratitude."

The years between the wars saw a rapid expansion of Swedish industry, the rebuilding of the Norwegian merchant marine, and the further development of Norway's industries and, in Denmark, the adoption of a system of cooperative agriculture which has made her one of the world's largest exporters of dairy products, bacon, and ham. All the Scandinavian nations suffered from the slump which began in 1929, but much less severely than many of their European neighbors.

The coming of Hitler to supreme power in Germany in 1933 and the encroachments first upon the liberties of his own people and then on those of other countries which the Führer subsequently organized were viewed by Scandinavian governments with resigned apprehension. They placed their hopes of being left in peace in their formally declared policy of neutrality. However, as one of the more realistic Swedish commentators pointed out, these declarations had about as much value as a treaty between a hungry wolf and a small lamb.

In April, 1940, when the war between Germany and France and Great Britain was eight months old, the wolf gobbled up two lambs in a single bite. The Danes, demobilized and quite unable to resist the Nazi onslaught, had been the only Scandinavian country to sign a non-aggression pact with Germany. Perhaps somewhat reassured by Hitler's promises to respect their law and customs, they yielded to the German invasion almost without a struggle. Military matters were immediately taken over, but the government and Christian X were to continue to function as usual. Though Christian continued to make his daily rides unescorted through the streets of Copenhagen as an inspiration to his subjects, and though he urged the people to remain calm, he personally defied the Germans on a number of occasions.

Norway fought the invaders with the support of a British naval and military force which, as was usual with the British at that stage in the war, proved to be too little and too late. Nevertheless the Norwegian and British forces put up a remarkably stiff resistance which went far toward temporarily crippling the German navy and took a heavy toll of German troops. Elderly King Haakon established a government in exile in England. He contemptuously rejected a German demand for concessions which would have been unconstitutional and told his ministers, who were inclined to be timid in the face of German aggressive-

Tivoli, illuminated nightly by some 100,000 bulbs, is Copenhagen's world-famous playground. Shown here, the fanciful Pagoda Restaurant.

ness, that they might do what they chose but that he, for his part, would abdicate if Hitler's terms were accepted. This threat rallied the government, and Haakon became the symbol and standard-bearer of Norwegian resistance. Nevertheless, Nazi rule was imposed and local sympathizers, like Vidkun Quisling, were placed in charge. The occupation, unlike that in Denmark, was costly.

Only Sweden, richest and most populous of the Scandinavian kingdoms, escaped invasion, and she did so by making just enough concessions to Germany to ensure respect for her neutrality. One of these concessions, which has never been forgiven by the Norwegians, was to allow the German army the use of Swedish railroads for the transport of troops, arms, and supplies to Norway; nor did the Swedish attitude toward Denmark give the people of that country much pleasure. Although Swedish public opinion was much less favorable to Hitler than it had been to Kaiser William II, it was, in the earlier years of the war, equivocal toward the Allies, to say the least. This was not the case, however, in the great port of Göteborg, where feelings were uncompromisingly anti-Nazi. (Stockholmers were wont to say, with a slight sneer, that whenever it rained in London the people of Göteborg immediately put up their umbrellas as in sympathy.)

Scandinavia's only republic had already had a savage baptism by fire from another quarter. In November, 1939, Russia made certain territorial demands on Finland, ostensibly in self-protection against the future intentions of Germany, at that time an uncomfortable ally of the U.S.S.R. The Finns promptly rejected the Russian demands, whereupon, on November 30, Russian forces marched across the Finnish frontier, headed by bands playing cheerful march tunes and, for some reason, confident of a hearty welcome from the Finns. The Finnish army, under the veteran Marshal Mannerheim, gave the Russians a warm welcome indeed: most of the invading force was annihilated, to the astonishment of the Soviet rulers in Moscow, who were forced to throw more and more troops into Finland during the bitter four months of what is now called the "Winter War."

At last, after standing quite alone against the might of the Soviet Union, the Finns were forced by sheer weight of numbers to capitulate on March 30, 1940. In June, 1941, however, Finland joined Germany in declaring war on Russia. Although the Finns never regarded themselves as allies of Germany, they fought their so-called "Continuation War" for three years, until, in September, 1944, the Soviet Union agreed to an armistice on surprisingly lenient terms. Meanwhile, the events of the Winter War and of Finnish-German cooperation thereafter were also bound to confirm Sweden's decision to remain neutral rather than to risk all in joining the Allies.

In the meanwhile, organized resistance in Norway and Denmark, actively aided by Britain and later by the United States, was beginning to assume formidable proportions. This was especially the case in Norway, whose geography and climate were admirably suited to guerrilla warfare. Thanks to the activities of local resistance forces and threats of invasion by sea, no fewer than 600,000 German troops were needed to occupy Norway and were consequently diverted from the major battle theaters elsewhere. And the Norwegian merchant navy once again gave invaluable help to the allied cause.

In Denmark resistance was slower to gain momentum and more difficult to organize. Denmark was, according to Hitler's original plan, to have been Germany's model "protectorate," and at first every effort was made by the Nazis to show Danes the best side of their natures. But as victory seemed to elude Hitler, the genial mask began to slip.

When Christian responded to a birthday telegram from Hitler with a curt thank you note, it was received as a most unacceptable example of Danish insubordination. The German ambassador to Copenhagen was instructed to tell Christian that "a king of Denmark is in no position to reply to the Führer of the Greater German Reich in such a way." On August 28, 1943, when the government refused to declare a state of emergency at Germany's bidding, Nazi troops took over key buildings and imprisoned many leaders. From then on Denmark was under still tighter rein. Jews were persecuted, Danes of all religious persuasions were enrolled for forced labor in Germany, and the occupation grew daily more oppressive. Resistance correspondingly became more widespread and active. The Danish Freedom Council, established in the summer of 1943, put the movement on a military footing, and the council became the supreme authority for all Danes except the handful of traitors whom the Germans had managed to win over. Under their leadership some six thousand Jews escaped to Sweden aboard coastal police vessels and fishing boats; massive strikes were

called; and plans for post-war restoration of order were set in motion.

On May 7, 1945, Germany surrendered. Sweden had come through the war intact, and for this its Danish and Norwegian neighbors have not quite given their pardon. King Haakon VII returned in triumph to Norway and set about the rebuilding of his country. King Christian X of Denmark was at last free to do the same—he had insisted throughout the war on being treated as a prisoner-of-war by the Germans. Finland had made concessions to Russia, but she was still free and, by extraordinary diplomatic skill, she was not Communist.

The years which have passed since the guns of World War II fell silent have seen Scandinavia make great strides. Norway and Denmark are members of the North Atlantic Treaty Organization. Sweden is not, but she has one of the largest air forces in the world, an extremely powerful navy, and can put a large army into the field at any time.

The progress made by Swedish industry, thanks largely to an extremely intelligently organized system of labor relations, has been remarkable, and the Swedish standard of living is probably the highest (and one of the most expensive) in the world. If you ask any Swede about taxation he will wince perhaps a shade more than the citizens of other nations, for he pays the highest rate in the West—but all those ships and aircraft cost money. So do highly developed social services, including hospitalization, education, and pension systems, in which Sweden leads the world in many respects.

As has already been mentioned, Sweden made up for her lack of coal, the classic nineteenth-century source of power, by the massive generation of electricity, using the force of water to drive the generators. Nor was this development as costly as it has been elsewhere, since Sweden's countless lakes have been used as natural reservoirs and the building of great dams has therefore been largely unnecessary. Apart from the rich store of iron ore in the north, which is one of the mainstays of the Swedish economy, Sweden has made the most of the vast forests, which still cover half the country, to build up a flourishing timber industry, great paper mills, the world's largest match industry, and the manufacture of prefabricated houses and fashionable furniture. Quite distinctive, too, is the Swedish glass industry, though this is an old established craft, the first glassworks at Kosta, in Småland, having been founded in 1741. Today the Orrefors Works produces glassware

"The Cry," a lithograph by Edvard Munch of Norway, eloquently expresses the dark, brooding aspect of the Scandinavian character.

of every kind, from milk bottles to hand-cut crystal and decorative pieces, which are complemented on the dinner table by the beautiful stainless steel cutlery whose makers vie with the shipbuilders of Göteborg for the ore which comes from Kiruna and Gällivare.

Norway, its flag once more seen wherever ships go, now possesses a merchant fleet of almost twenty million tons, the sixth largest in the world. The nation has, if possible, made even better use of water power than has Sweden. Its rushing rivers are capable of producing thirty million kilowatts of electricity, of which about a third is actually consumed today. This represents more electricity per head of population than is furnished by any other country in the world, and Norway uses it to power its massive aluminum industry and large factories which produce artificial fertilizers. Since fish has always been a staple of the Norwegian economy it is not surprising that a massive canning and deep-freezing industry should have been set up or that a modern mechanized fishing fleet has largely supplanted the independent fisherman.

Norway lost her beloved King Haakon VII in 1957 and he was succeeded by the hardly less popular King Olaf V, who was born in 1903 and was married to the late Princess Märta of Sweden. When, in 1950, Sweden's Gustaf V died, he was followed on the throne by King Gustaf VI, twice married and twice a widower. Of King Gustaf's four sons, the eldest, Prince Gustaf Adolf, duke of Västerbotten, was killed in an air crash in 1947, and two others have given up their royal rights by morganatic marriages. The present heir to the Swedish throne is Crown Prince Carl Gustaf, the son of the late Prince Gustaf Adolf.

The former king of Denmark, Frederick IX, who was born in 1899 and succeeded his father in 1947, died in January, 1972. He had no sons and so, by a special law passed in 1953, he was succeeded by his elder daughter, now Queen Margrethe.

Some apology is due, perhaps, for this summary of present day Scandinavian royalty, but we have seen so many kings and queens pass across the pages of this book that it is only right to bring the record up to date. For it is largely through and because of crowned heads that the story of the Scandinavian nations has come to pass, with their successes and failures, their achievements and falls from grace. Yet behind all these crowned figures who move with varying degrees of stateliness through the story stand the people without whom they would have

The aerial view of a Copenhagen suburb in which village intimacy is sought through the arrangement of houses in small, boulevard-free clusters.

been nothing. Their work may be admired in the Scandinavia of today, which they and their rulers have fashioned.

Of all Scandinavians, the Danes have been traditionally the most dependent upon agriculture for their livelihood. Even today, although only 14 per cent of the people are still engaged in farming, almost 75 per cent of the land remains under cultivation, an extraordinarily high proportion in this last third of the twentieth century. Some eighty years ago the Danish government set about reclaiming the barren moorlands of Jutland and these once useless acres are now fertile. At the same time a start was made with the establishment of farming cooperatives, which undertook the processing and marketing of many farms in each area and the introduction of intensive systems of livestock management. Today Danish butter, eggs, pork products, bacon, and cheese are the economic backbone of the country.

Industry engages another 30 per cent of the population, for perhaps even more than Sweden the Danes have interested themselves and the rest of the world in industrial arts. Royal Copenhagen porcelain is cherished in every part of the world, and early in the present century the work of the silversmith Georg Jensen began to be world famous, as it still is under Jensen's former apprentice, Kaj Bojesen. Denmark is also a leader in the production of beautiful modern furniture, notwithstanding her lack of native wood. Here the great designer Kaare Klint led the way fifty years ago and his designs have been guidelines of this Danish industry ever since.

About one third of the Finnish economy is dependent upon industry—metals, mining, machine-tool manufacturing, engineering, food processing, paper and paper products, furniture, textiles, and chemicals—another 15 per cent upon agriculture, including forestry. But perhaps Finland's most distinctive contributions to the modern world are found in her architecture and in her ceramics. Alvar Aalto and Eliel Saarinen (father of Eero Saarinen, who made his reputation in the United States) rank among the twentieth century's leading creative designers. New communities such as Tapiola have provided models for imaginative urban design in other countries. The great Arabia Ceramic Factory, which will soon mark its centenary, dominates the ceramics industry in both utilitarian and artistic products, and employs designers who have become celebrated in Scandinavia and elsewhere.

How do social achievements of Scandinavia's nations stand today?
They have in common a deep respect for human rights, a mistrust of hasty change hardly less deep (all modern "permissiveness" notwithstanding), and a love of the institutions of government which have proved their worth. That is why three of the four nations are still monarchies. At the same time, the Scandinavian nations are sincerely democratic, in the proper sense of that much-abused word, and they have proved—a lesson which other larger countries might take to heart—that a large measure of state control can go hand in hand with private enterprise. (A small but outspoken minority of Scandinavians, especially in Sweden, see this massive welfare system as a threat to individual freedom, but most people support the general trend toward governmental protectionism.)

No countries are more humanitarian than those of Scandinavia nor have better laws for the protection of the workers, mothers, children, and old people. Few people in Scandinavia are extremely rich and none extremely poor. Class warfare and strikes are almost unknown, thanks to enlightened labor relations. A minimum of seven years of education is standardized and compulsory for all, and advanced training equivalent to high school, college, and vocational schools is also provided free. Military service is also compulsory for men, since it is an ancient tradition in Scandinavia, already noted in this book, that the citizen has obligations to the state, as the state has toward him.

Although parliamentary government in the full sense was only achieved in the last century, it at once put out strong roots, which is more than can be said for many other nations. Only in Finland, for obvious reasons, has Communism made any impact, in spite of a degree of press freedom liberal even by American standards. As the Swedes say: *"En ann är så god som en ann"*—"Everyone is as good as everyone else," and this proverb may be taken as the motto of modern Scandinavia.

On the tomb of Sir Christopher Wren, the rebuilder of London after the Great Fire of 1666, is the inscription: *Si monumentum requiris, circumspice*—"If you seek a monument, look around you." Scandinavia today is the monument to all her past builders. Perhaps a few readers will feel that they would like to look around the monument whose building I have described. They will be well rewarded if they do so.

OVERLEAF: *Here Swedish miners enjoy a lunchtime respite beneath Persberg, where iron mines have been operating since the fifteenth century.*

CHRONOLOGY

10,000 B.C.	Evidence of Old Stone Age hunters in Denmark
2500	Archaeological finds indicate agricultural settlements
1000–500	Bronze Age relics reveal highly artistic pagan culture
A.D. 1–100	A seafaring import and export society develops
793–1000	Vikings attack Lindisfarne, inaugurating two centuries of piracy, marauding, trade, and emigration to other lands
829	Monk Ansgar introduces Christianity
872	Harold the Fairhaired becomes first supreme ruler of Norway
1016	King Canute completes conquest of southern Norway and England
1066	Battle of Hastings brings Normans to English throne.
1157–1241	Valdemars' rule in Denmark brings unity among provinces; Bishop Absalon founds Copenhagen; Danish flag created
1250	Birger Jarl, founder of Folkung dynasty, builds Stockholm
1282	*Handfaestning,* The Great Charter, establishes Swedish parliament
1332–1370	German Hanseatic League dominates Baltic commerce; Black Plague depopulates Norwegian peasantry, dooms feudalism
1397	Union of Kalmar uneasily unites Denmark, Sweden, and Norway
1435	Engelbrekt calls first meeting of Swedish Riksdag, in Arboga
1480	Printing press introduced at newly founded Uppsala University
1500s	The Reformation reaches Scandinavia
1520	Christian II takes reprisals against Swedish rebels in the Stockholm blood bath; Gustavus Vasa leads Swedish peasants in overthrow of Danish rule, establishes Vasa dynasty
1534	Civil wars result in strengthened aristocracy and Lutheranism
1550s	Expansion of trade and commerce in Scandinavia
1563–1570	The Great Northern Seven Years' War pits Denmark against Sweden
1588–1648	Christian IV promotes flowering of arts in Sweden, modernizes military and commercial system, creates new cities
1611–1613	In renewal of wars, Swedish armies overwhelm Danish
1632	Gustavus II Adolphus killed in Battle of Lützen
1644	Queen Christina abdicates Swedish throne to Palatinate rule
1648	Treaty of Westphalia assigns part of northern Germany to Sweden
1657–1660	Danish-Swedish War results in territorial losses for Denmark
1660–1670	Frederick III's enlightened absolutism modernizes Denmark
1709	Charles XII's early successful plans for Swedish expansion meet Russian opposition, ending in defeat at Battle of Poltava
1718	Charles XII killed during Swedish invasion of Norway

1718–1772	The Estates replace monarchical tyranny as Sweden enters Age of Freedom with a new constitution and party rule
1721	Peace of Nystad ends Swedish domination of Baltic
1786	Swedish Academy established as literary force
1788	Ascription of Swedish peasants abolished; social and agricultural reforms inaugurated
1801	Sweden, Denmark, and Norway ally with Russia against England in Napoleonic War strategies; Admiral Nelson engages Danish fleet in battle to break neutrality pact
1807	British bombard Copenhagen, driving Denmark into alliance with Napoleon against Sweden, Britain, and Russia in Seven Years' War; Sweden cedes Finland to Russia
1813	Frederick VI makes peace with Sweden; Denmark loses much land but retains Iceland, Greenland, and Faroe Islands; in Sweden Charles XIV John establishes Bernadotte dynasty
1814	Peace of Kiel places Norway under Swedish royal rule, but retains autonomous constitution and parliament
1849	Frederick VII of Denmark signs Constitution on June 5
1850s	Crop failures in Sweden and Norway and poverty of landless farm workers set off wave of immigration to U.S.
1864	Denmark fights Austria and Prussia over territorial claims
1895	Alfred Nobel, Swedish explosives manufacturer, endows foundation dedicated to peace and humanitarian achievements
1899	Russification program in Finland creates backlash there
1901	In Denmark *de facto* parliamentary government is introduced
1914–1918	All three monarchies maintain neutrality during World War I; Finland declared a republic December 6, 1917
1915	Danish women granted suffrage
1918	Iceland becomes a kingdom in personal union with Denmark
1930s	Social reforms in Denmark introduced; Finland struggles to maintain independent neutrality but is considered a German ally
1940	Denmark and then Norway are attacked and occupied by Nazis; Sweden manages to remain outside conflict of World War II
1944	Iceland dissolves personal union with Denmark; Finland breaks off relations with Germany, accepts Allies' armistice terms
1945	German occupation of Scandinavia ends May 5; Sweden, Norway, and Denmark join United Nations
1949	Denmark and Norway join NATO
1953	A new constitution for Denmark signed by king; Nordic council for economic, social, and cultural cooperation is ratified by Scandinavian countries
1955	Finland admitted to United Nations
1960	Denmark joins European Free Trade Alliance
1972	Queen Margrethe II ascends Danish throne
1972	Denmark plans to leave EFTA and join EEC although other Scandinavian countries are undecided or negative about becoming members of the Common Market

CREDITS AND INDEX

Page numbers in **boldface type** refer to illustrations.
Page references to map entries are in *italic type*.